ALSO BY DIANE REHM

*Finding My Voice*

# Toward
# Commitment

# Toward Commitment

*A Dialogue About Marriage*

## Diane Rehm

*and*

## John B. Rehm

Alfred A. Knopf   *New York*   2002

THIS IS A BORZOI BOOK
PUBLISHED BY ALFRED A. KNOPF

www.aaknopf.com

Knopf, Borzoi Books, and the colophon are registered trademarks
of Random House, Inc.

A brief excerpt from this work was previously
published in *Modern Maturity*.

Library of Congress Cataloging-in-Publication Data
Rehm, Diane.
Toward commitment : a dialogue about marriage / Diane Rehm and
John B. Rehm.
p.  cm.
ISBN 0-375-41430-4 (alk. paper)
1. Marriage—United States.   2. Man-woman relationships—United States.
3. Rehm, Diane.   4. Rehm, John B.   I. Rehm, John B.   II. Title.

HQ536 R4339 2002
306.81'0973—dc21        2002025483

Manufactured in the United States of America
Published October 2, 2002
Second Printing, December 2002

*We dedicate our book to*


*David, Nancy, and Alex*

*and*

*Jennie, Russell, Benjamin,*

*and Sarah*

# Contents

*Introduction*                                    *ix*

Assumptions and Expectations                        3

Diane's and John's Appeal                          18

Anger                                              29

Family                                             39

Making Love                                        50

Solitude                                           59

Money                                              70

Profession                                         82

Religion                                           94

Parenting                                         104

Arguing                                           114

Friends                                           123

Vacations                                         131

Criticism                                         142

Psychotherapy                           153

Retirement                              163

The Other Partner as Professional       172

Holiday Celebrations                    185

Illness                                 193

Food                                    204

In-Laws                                 215

Sleep                                   227

The Third Person                        234

Aging                                   245

Grandparenting                          257

Death                                   266

Conclusion                              275

*Appendix*                              279

*Acknowledgments*                       287

# Introduction

The idea for this book grew out of a series of radio broadcasts we did nearly twenty years ago on a variety of issues facing all couples who attempt to build and strengthen a healthy relationship. The subjects of those broadcasts included dependence and independence in marriage, attitudes toward money, dealing with anger, and handling religious or spiritual differences. The series drew widespread attention, with many requests for cassette copies. Letters and phone calls came in to WAMU-FM, the public radio station in Washington, D.C., for which Diane works, indicating that couples, families, and even neighborhood groups were using the cassettes as starting points for their own discussions of marriage and family issues.

As we toured the country together talking about Diane's earlier book, *Finding My Voice,* many people approached her, thanking her for the honesty with which she'd written about our marriage, the difficulties we've faced, and how we've managed to work our way through them. There are very few, if any, books that speak honestly, from a nonprofessional point of view, about the realities of relationships. In a sense, the two of us have become "professionals," struggling both individually and together through long periods of therapy, questioning why each of us is who we are, what we have in common, how to move toward bridging the gaps, and how to move toward acceptance of those gaps that will never be bridged.

We have written a two-person narrative about the ups and downs of a forty-two-year relationship. Our book is intended not only for married persons but for all people striving to live together and stay together. We speak from our perspective as a married couple, but we believe that our experiences, including the difficulties we faced and our ultimate decision to remain together, can be applied to those engaged in unmarried relationships, deep friendships, and same-sex partnerships.

We have written about our backgrounds, what brought us together, our expectations of marriage, the difficulties and rewards of coming to "know" each other, raising children, addressing financial, religious, and social needs, different styles of communication, and how we've persevered through the really rugged down times. In particular, we have addressed twenty-six topics. In each case, there are two brief essays, one by John and one by Diane, and then a dialogue between the two of us.

We have tried to combine both humorous and serious passages to underscore the idea that marriage—or any long-term relationship—is a never-ending process of exploration and growth. We have drawn on and shared our own experiences, and included advice offered to us by a number of professionals, both pastoral counselors and psychotherapists, with whom we have been privileged to work over many of these forty-two years.

One example: during one of our particularly difficult periods, when we could barely speak to each other without hostility in our voices, our counselor suggested we write and sign a contract agreeing, among other things, *to be totally uncritical of each other.* The first clause said, "I will be totally uncritical of my spouse. I will not utter a single critical word. I will allow myself to experience how that feels." We have included a copy of the entire contract following the chapter entitled "Criticism." For two people who'd been criticizing each other constantly, it was not an easy thing to write, to agree to, to sign, or to stick to. But that contract, and the three that followed over the next ten months, got us over another big hump.

If this book succeeds in provoking individuals to think harder and more seriously about the committed relationship, both its benefits and its drawbacks, it will have been worthwhile.

# Toward
# Commitment

# Assumptions and Expectations

## John

Looking back to the time before our wedding in December 1959, I am shocked by the naïveté of the assumptions I held about the experience we call marriage. In the ardor of intimacy, sexual and otherwise, I gave little thought to what lay ahead. I assumed that children, in some indeterminate number, would come, and that a family would emerge therefrom. I further assumed that, as a hardworking and ambitious young lawyer, I would see my income steadily rise and would come to afford a decent standard of living. Most tellingly, I assumed that Diane and I would establish a mutually rewarding relationship, with no special efforts by, or demands upon, me. In short, the way we lived together in the first year of our marriage, before our son, David, arrived, would, in some deterministic fashion, serve as the model for our coexistence thereafter.

These assumptions concealed deep and even dark questions that I would be forced to face in later years, especially in therapy.

How would I deal with my strong inclination at times to be alone and withdraw from others?

How would I become sensitive to Diane's need for intimacy beyond sexual gratification? How would I achieve a reasonable balance between the conflicting demands of family and profession? Above all, how would I learn enough about myself to develop into a warm and understanding husband and father?

In short, coasting on easy assumptions, I failed to articulate—to myself and others—any realistic expectations about the many facets of marriage. Unlike assumptions, expectations lend themselves to discussion with the other partner, and thereby to adjustment and accommodation. Assumptions, which by nature tend to be concealed and static, are traps that I fell into. Expectations, on the other hand, can serve as a foundation for a dynamic relationship. At the time, however, it never occurred to me to share my expectations with Diane.

In the absence of articulated and shared expectations, I—and we—blundered upon important truths about ourselves. This process of trial and error proved to be inefficient and emotionally costly. In time, therapy proved to offer a far better way of identifying problems and trying to attack them. At the very least, therapy gave me the support and guidance I needed to become a constructive partner in our marriage. But I am struck by the price we paid for the ignorance with which I entered into our relationship.

# Diane

Having been married once before, I did come to our marriage with both assumptions and expectations. My first assumption was that this marriage was forever. I vowed to myself that divorce would never again be a factor in my life. I assumed I had learned enough about myself—and how to live with another person—through that failure, that I would be a perfect partner to John. After all, I told myself, I was no longer the same person who had married at nineteen. I was now a "mature" twenty-three. I had lost my parents. I had successfully lived on my own for the first time in my life. I had virtually separated myself from my community of origin here in Washington. I assumed that, because of those experiences, I had become a wiser, more independent person.

John and I enjoyed a wonderful romance, what every young woman dreams of. He was warm, sweet, kind, and attentive. On one of our very first dinner dates, I developed a terrible stomachache, perhaps a result of nervousness at being with the first man I'd dated since the divorce. I was embarrassed, but to my total surprise, John exhibited a kindness and caring I'd never before experienced, even from my own parents.

We went to concerts, to plays, to art galleries, to movies. We went on long walks, talking constantly, glancing at each other, shyly kissing for the first time in the boxwood gardens at the home of George Mason. We loved taking long drives into the countryside and then going out for pizza and wine at Luigi's, talking about our dreams, our fantasies, our attraction to each other. *In vino veritas,* John said to me, and then had to translate.

I naively believed I understood how to deal with tensions in personal relationships because I had undergone a three-year marriage and the trauma of divorce. So much of what my ex-husband and I brought to our marriage was based on similarities: culture, language, status. Our families knew one another, we came from the same community, we enjoyed the same foods, we understood our heritage. There were good times, of course. For the most part, however, those good times were not spent by ourselves, but rather when we were with friends, sharing laughter and good food.

When the breakup came, after the death of my parents, I knew in my heart that, as much as leaving my husband, I wanted to leave that very same community which had surrounded me for my whole life. I yearned for freedom from the familiar, and my search—both internal and external—was leading me in directions I sensed would allow me to experience that freedom.

When John Rehm came into my life, I believed that he represented all of those "new directions" I was seeking but unable to articulate: a broad worldly outlook, sophistication in music and art, and sensitivity to each and every aspect of my mood, my tone, my actions. When he finally came around to proposing (and writing it down!) I accepted because I knew marriage to John would bring with it an entrée into "the world" that I had never before experienced.

Of course, I also saw in John a tendency to withdraw, to separate himself from me, to "close down." However, I convinced myself that whatever the causes of such episodes—lasting moments or hours—they would magically disappear if we were married. He was, to my eyes, *perfect*.

# Dialogue on Assumptions and Expectations

DIANE: The whole question of marriage revolves around assumptions and expectations. I was twenty-two, you were twenty-nine, and we never talked about such ideas. I don't know how that might have affected how we behaved toward each other. What do you think?

JOHN: Well, I think it would've made for an easier relationship, because we would have shared plans, shared commitments, a sense of where both parties were going, instead of making up the decisions as we went along. I think it would have been a more stable foundation for a marriage.

DIANE: But you had this whole external set of expectations. Number one, that you would be "in charge" of the family. Number two, that you would be the breadwinner. Number three, that I would take care of the household and the children. And, of course, I shared those expectations. Mine were no different from yours. The area where we differed was in our internal lives: how much I expected you to be a partner to me, and how much you expected to be solitary. That's where the expectations and the anticipations differed.

JOHN: Yes, I agree, and that's where I think the expectations move into the trickier realm that I call assumptions, because the expectations you've just mentioned rested upon my own personality, which had never been tested, because I'd never lived with anybody else before. It took some years for me to gain at least some understanding of who I was in that respect, and that's of course where therapy helped. So it's particularly the area of assumptions, unstated assumptions of which we're largely ignorant, that I think was the most troublesome aspect of our marriage.

DIANE: Beyond that, because I did not understand your unstated need, the first year after David was born, you assumed that we were not going to make it. You said to me at that point, do you remember, "I'm not sure we've made the right marriage."

JOHN: I don't recall the specific instance, but I'm not surprised, because for me, how shall I say it, this marriage was a brand-new, unforeseen test of who I was and how I could get along with others. That need had never arisen in my life before. My parents were happy to have me lead a solitary life if that's what I wanted and to follow that course for the rest of my life.

DIANE: But why did you get married in the first place then?

JOHN: Good question. Sexual desire was, without question, a powerful motive.

DIANE: But you could've had sexual relations with other women.

JOHN: That's certainly true. But somewhere in me, obviously, there was a desire for a more permanent commitment, something I could count on, and I suppose that's another one of the unstated assumptions, lurking below the surface, that I made. In a sense, though paradoxical, I needed some degree of security as well as, within that security, the freedom to be on my own. That's quite a tension.

DIANE: And that's where we got into trouble. Because you had the security of coming home to me every single night, or, as the need arose, you said, "I have to work. I have to work six days a week. I have to work seven days a week." So that I was left thinking and feeling, Well, my God, where is he in this marriage? And your excuse was *always* work!

JOHN: You've put your finger on it. I was both in and out of the marriage at the same time. Or that's what I *wanted,* to be in and out of the marriage at my choosing. So that, when I wanted to, I would have a companion, beautiful, sexually attractive. At other times I would leave the house, primarily through work, but in other ways as well, as they occurred to me.

DIANE: Do you think other young men behave in similar ways? Do you think you're *that* different from other young men, not only of your generation but of this generation?

JOHN: Well, not that different, though I may be a bit farther along the spectrum. As you and I have discussed before, I am convinced that there's something in the male psyche which does make it difficult to make that commitment. Our literature, culture, movies, are full of instances where young men are dragged into marriage, on the one hand thinking that it's what society expects, but on the other hand resenting it, resenting the loss of freedom that marriage entails. I think many—perhaps *most*—men go through that, at some level. I think we've known male friends who've been able to balance the two reasonably well, and other cases, not so well.

DIANE: You and I have seen instances in the last ten years where parents have spent hundreds of thousands of dollars on weddings, and then the couples have divorced or separated within a year or so. Do you think that if I had somehow not been as committed as I was to the relationship, you would've said, "Well, this didn't quite work out the way I wanted, so I'll help support the child, but goodbye"?

John: I think there's a good chance that that would've happened. I've long felt, and I've said to you several times, that your almost irrational commitment to the relationship, growing out of your own prior relationship, is what sustained our relationship at its darkest moments, and that, given my free choice—it's not that clear to me, but there's certainly a good chance that I would've walked away, because I simply was not making, and was not prepared to make, that fundamental commitment to the marriage.

Diane: But what did that fundamental commitment constitute in your own mind? That word "commitment" comes up so often, and yet I'm not quite sure I have an understanding of what the word means to you, what it might mean to other people—other men, especially. You hear young women say, again and again, "This man is not willing to make a commitment." What did that mean to you?

John: For me, commitment meant a dedication to our family, which at times would override, and should override, my own desire to be off by myself, doing things by myself. It was a little easier for me to do so because you were fighting so hard to keep the marriage together. We've been talking about some of the problems I had in making a commitment and what that means. I'd like to ask you, from where do you think came the strength of your desire for commitment, your ability to make a commitment—where did all that come from?

Diane: Well, first of all, deep down, I think I knew I married a good man, though there were times when I was angry, I was frustrated, I was beyond belief at your behavior, at your lack of interest, at your failure to even be part of the family for long periods of time. But remember also that, having been married once before, I was absolutely determined that this marriage was going to be a lifetime commitment. You know, you and I fell in love, and a year later we were married—we didn't really know each other. But I felt this was a marriage worth having, that our first child, our son, was so beautiful, and such a gift from heaven, and that we had a family worth having. I knew you were a dedicated worker, I knew you were loyal, I knew you were committed to the *idea* of supporting this family that you had, materially but not yet emotionally, and I knew that that was going to be the long-term challenge, to find for both of us that balance. Of course, there was the economic underpinning, but where was the emotional underpinning? That's what I was committed, in a sense, to find.

JOHN: Even at the worst times, you still had something you could rely upon, that sustained you? That sounds truly irrational, when you look at all the considerations at the time, and the nature of my behavior. Why persist in an almost masochistic fashion?

DIANE: Don't get me wrong. There were many times when I thought, I can't stand this anymore. I'm going to leave him! I'm going to find an apartment. I'm going to take the baby and live on my own. But still, I felt it was important—and by that time Jennie had come along—I felt these two children needed two parents. Now, that's very different from the thinking today, but that is my old-fashioned—

JOHN: But suppose the husband in question is behaving in a destructive fashion, destructive to the family? Then what? Surely there's no point in maintaining—

DIANE: I think you're absolutely right.

JOHN: Did you reach that point in our relationship?

DIANE: No, because I think the fundamentals were there. We were economically supported. You loved the children—that was clear. When you were around, you maintained a wonderful relationship with both of them. My complaint was that you were not there often enough, and when you were there, frankly, you were more engaged with the children than you were with me. Or else you were sleeping, claiming fatigue, or claiming that you didn't have the energy for anything.

JOHN: It sounds as though you were willing to accept a pretty barren—that may be an overstatement—barren relationship for the sake of something you hoped or believed would evolve in the future. You were trading a lot of present pain for a future hope of a better time. I think someone of the younger generation would say, "Boy, this doesn't sound like a very good deal to me. . . . Why continue this way? Why not just go our separate ways?"

DIANE: We're back to anticipations and expectations. In my culture, OK, you make a mistake once, that may be acceptable. Everybody can make a mistake once. But to make a mistake twice, when you've got children involved, seemed to me totally unacceptable. And then you have to understand that my pride wouldn't allow me to accept a second failure. I didn't want to suffer the humiliation that would've been involved. To be off on my own, as a single woman, with two children, was not the accepted norm at that time, and was not something I would've felt I could have done for myself. Remember that there was economic security.

JOHN: But we didn't have much money then.

DIANE: It *was* enough to meet our needs, though, especially since

neither one of us was a spendthrift. I felt comforted and protected by a sense of security that I didn't have growing up or
in my first marriage.

JOHN: Then let me change the question a little bit. Suppose you
hadn't had a prior marriage and that you hadn't been driven
by this fierce desire to keep the marriage going. Would that
have changed things?

DIANE: Probably. But who knows? The presence of children
changed things for me. In my first marriage, there were no
children. And I had no real compunction about leaving that
marriage, because it was totally unsatisfying: economically,
physically, socially—in just about every way. He is a good
man, but we were not compatible. I knew from our first year
together that there was a human being inside you with whom
I could connect.

JOHN: But don't you think it comes down to the question of how
much pain is worth enduring for the sake of a better future?
I think that's where the younger generation says—not unrea-
sonably, perhaps—if commitment entails this trade-off, why
should I get involved at all? It sounds as though it involves too
many present problems for the sake of a somewhat evanes-
cent future. How would you advise somebody who poses that
question?

DIANE: I'm not going to advise anybody. What I do think is that
today's woman is far more independent in her economic status, professional status, and social status. She is far more free
to make the choices that she makes. My concern is that both
men and women go into marriage without a true sense of
commitment. In the case of a physically abusive relationship,
I think there are probably no ways that a couple can make it.

That was never the case in our relationship. I was turning to other pursuits, you remember. We bought a piano. We bought a sewing machine. I began to turn to those things literally with a passion . . . a passion that I would have loved to bestow on you, but you weren't receptive at that point in our lives.

JOHN: In a sense, what you and I are talking about is a kind of unwritten question: Is there any reason why the traditional marriage, consisting of a nuclear family, a husband, a wife, children, should continue to exist? Maybe we don't need it anymore. Maybe right now, we're all searching for alternative ways of living together.

DIANE: I think you're right. I think the world is searching for other ways. Women living more independently, alone with their children—sometimes by choice, sometimes by neglect, or simply because of pregnancy in an unmarried situation. I continue, perhaps out of my old-fashioned beliefs, to feel that a child needs two people. Whether those people are married, whether they're the same sex, whether they're simply living together, I feel that a child needs two parents. Just one parent doesn't do the trick, because there needs to be a reflection from that other parent. Plus, frankly, I agree with Hillary Clinton's statement that it does "take a village" to raise a child. It took not only you and me, our different perspectives, our different perceptions, it took the schools they went to, their friends, the parents of the friends, our own friends—it took a whole broad spectrum of people to raise our children in health. At that time I strongly believed it took at least two people—in our case, a man and a woman.

JOHN: The thing that so strikes me about this awkward and difficult process is how it does rest upon this fundamental ignorance of who we are. What overwhelms me after years of marriage is that we entered into this relationship with gross ignorance of ourselves and the other. In a sense, I suppose I might suggest that an enduring marriage is one that continues to explore and reveal the ignorance. It never goes away. There are times when I live with you as a stranger. I hardly recognize you. At other times, I feel intimately close to you with some strong sense of who you are.

DIANE: And what makes the difference? Do you know?

JOHN: No. . . . I'm almost tempted to say the weather. It's so subtle, and of course, I also do believe that we're all made up of an infinite range of different personalities, and sometimes the two mesh, and sometimes they don't, and there are degrees of meshing. It sort of oscillates. To appreciate the existence of the ignorance, to confess it and to share it, may be the beginning of an enduring relationship. No answers in the immediate sense.

DIANE: Just questions.

JOHN: Just questions. But you need the willingness and ability to state the questions . . . because that looks like weakness. . . .

DIANE: But what would you have asked me? What would I have asked you? I would have, instead of sitting quietly, said something like, "John, why are you so moody? Why are you so withdrawn at times? What is it about your personality that makes you this way?"

JOHN: To a far greater extent than I ever did, I would've sat down with you and said, "Diane, tell me something about your childhood. Was it happy? Sad? Why? What were your relationships with your mother and father?" It's taken me some years to get a really good sense as to the kind of almost alarming entity that your mother was, and the softer, gentler side that your father showed. Some understanding of who you were. Because who you were is who you are, to a large extent. That kind of anecdotal, historical reminiscence would have been very helpful.

DIANE: As I recall, either before we were married or shortly after we were married, we began talking about your mother and father. The fact that they slept at far ends of a hallway. The fact that you were quite often put in the middle in terms of mediating their relationship. I can't be sure that those revelations would've changed my view of who you were. And I'm not at all sure that I was really listening to what you were telling me—or that, at that point, I was actually equipped to listen.

JOHN: I think it would've given you a better understanding of my behavior and why I needed to go off and be by myself.

DIANE: And do you think that understanding some of this at that point would've made it easier for me?

JOHN: I think so.

DIANE: I think you may be right.

JOHN: And in terms of *your* childhood, as I've said, it's taken me years to get a clear picture of how your mother resonated inside you. . . .

DIANE: And still does.

JOHN: And that's a good point . . . how that continues to cling to you.

DIANE: To you as well: your father left you and your mother to go to war. Then your mother left you in Lynbrook to live with Aunt Katinka for a full year. You had this sense not only of being left alone but of *being* alone. And being, in some sense, abandoned by your mother. And abandoned by your father. You didn't see it that way then, but your mother was saying, "I have to go off and establish myself."

JOHN: And assuming you're right in using that term "abandoned," that probably only served to reinforce my desire and need to be alone.

DIANE: Talking about these assumptions and expectations does confirm how you and I entered into marriage in ignorance—ignorance of both ourselves and each other. Do you suppose we've spent our entire marriage in a process of trying to reduce that ignorance?

JOHN: Oh, I think so, particularly when we realize that the process never ends, and that some element of bedeviling ignorance will always be there.

DIANE: But the ignorance doesn't have to kill the marriage. Somehow, some *way,* we both knew—even if we didn't *know* we knew—that we had values we shared, such as caring about, and providing a good education for, our kids. If we had both understood how ignorant we were, we'd have been a heck of a lot better off.

# Diane's and John's Appeal

## John on Diane's Appeal

During our courtship, what drew me to Diane? We knew each other for about a year before our wedding. Over that time, I gained several powerful impressions of Diane, although they may have said more about me than her.

Nevertheless, right or wrong, those impressions combined to render her immensely desirable.

I first came to know Diane in 1958. She was secretary to a Foreign Service officer who was serving as a senior economic adviser in the State Department. I was a young lawyer assigned to a legal unit of the department. Her boss and I spent considerable time together backstopping the negotiation of the first economic assistance agreements with Algeria and Tunisia. In order to get to his office, I had to pass by Diane. We began warily to engage in brief and mundane conversations that masked—at least for me—strong feelings.

I had previously had scant experience with women. In high school, I participated in a few group dates. In college and law school, I probably had fewer than five real dates, which led to a few kisses and caresses but nothing more intimate. Although I admired and desired women, I was nevertheless easily unnerved by them. I was therefore unprepared for someone like Diane.

Physically, she was a knockout. Blond hair, a lovely face with a strong Semitic nose, full breasts, slim hips and legs. Combined, these features created an unmistakable allure. Her smallest gestures seemed sexually charged. As a result, I was especially nervous in her unavoidable presence, yet nevertheless intent upon pursuing her. That pursuit revealed other qualities that made her all the more desirable.

It became clear, for example, that Diane had a fierce intellectual curiosity. I soon learned that she had only a high school diploma and had never attended college. Yet on her desk were books like Dostoevski's *Brothers Karamazov,* Maugham's *Of Human Bondage,* and the essays of Alfred North Whitehead. It was obvious that she was tackling these and comparable books on her own. Her appetite for learning enabled me to play the role of mentor, reminiscent of the legend of Pygmalion. As my pupil, she became even more attractive.

There were other aspects of her desirability. At the time, she was separated from her husband and was increasingly determined to obtain a divorce. In my eyes, this made her both courageous and also somehow worldly. Moreover, she was of Arab extraction, her mother from Egypt and her father from Lebanon. This gave her an exotic aura. The fact that she was blond we laughingly attributed to an Anglo-Saxon crusader.

In short, in those heady days Diane was at one and the same

time physically beautiful, intellectually curious, worldly, and exotic. I have often said that I married her because of her lovely breasts and divine scrambled eggs. But how much did I really know about her? Very little, and probably no more than I knew about myself. Our mutual ignorance was, in retrospect, appalling, especially with regard to the dark sides of our upbringings. Yet that very ignorance probably allowed each of us—however unwisely—to follow our heart's desire.

In today's culture, the question arises whether we ever discussed the idea of living together for a trial period before marriage. To the best of my recollection, the idea never came up, I think for several reasons. First, we wanted a child as soon as possible, and we were not about to inflict illegitimacy on him or her. In addition, Diane's divorce made it all the more important to give our relationship the solemnity of a traditional marriage. Also, in 1959 the idea of just living together did not have the acceptance it does today. In short, cohabitation would not have fit in with our plans or suited our temperaments.

Would our marriage have gotten off to a better start if it had been preceded by, say, a year of living together? Or even having the experience of living with others? I am inclined to think it might have helped, because it could have provided an opportunity for greater understanding of ourselves. On the other hand, the very lack of a long-term commitment might have encouraged the deferral and even evasion of the tough issues.

# Diane on John's Appeal

To this day, I can remember my introduction to John Rehm (for some reason, throughout our marriage, I have always referred to John, or Scoop, as "John Rehm"—I have no idea why). I could hear him before I saw him. Even though the door to the hallway was closed, here came this booming voice, talking about legal issues pertaining to Africa. He walked into the office I shared with my boss at the Department of State, George Dolgin, who had already spoken to me in glowing terms about this brilliant young attorney with whom he was working.

John has always been youthful-looking. Back in 1958, he had a crew cut, he wore a simple blue button-down oxford shirt, a gray suit, and his shoes were shined. His physique was a football player's: very wide and muscular-looking shoulders, broad chest, all brought down through slim hips and long legs. All of which made for a very attractive young man. But his voice! It was overwhelming. I wanted to put my hands over my ears, but dared not insult this young man of whom my boss thought so highly. When he finally left the office, I breathed a sigh of relief.

He must have sensed my discomfort, because slowly, as he frequented the office, he began to talk more softly when he was speaking directly to me. He was flirtatious, but in a gentle way. We began talking about baseball, about which we were both passionate, each of us playing on the separate State Department teams for men and women. And finally, we made a bet on that year's World Series. John lost the bet and was therefore obligated to take me to dinner. He chose an old downtown restaurant,

Chez François, a small, intimate place known for its outstanding food, atmosphere, and service.

It was at this point that I began to appreciate and be attracted
to John Rehm. I can tell you what I wore that evening—a red
silk blouse and a black velvet skirt. John commented on my
attire, especially appreciating the color of my blouse. As we sat
down to dinner and began talking across a small table, I noticed
the beauty and fine lines of his hands, strong, large, and simply
and cleanly manicured. Why I am so drawn to hands I cannot
tell you, but I know they are one very important element I
observe as I meet individuals, and John's hands were and are
nothing short of beautiful.

I was also drawn to his interest in engaging in conversation,
his curiosity about various aspects of my life as well as his eager-
ness to share his own interests. He wore glasses, but behind them
were eyes that expressed warmth and kindness. He clearly knew
a lot about many different subjects. Whatever I asked him, he
seemed to be able to offer up an idea that enlightened me. He
asked about the books I was reading and why I had chosen them.
We had a marvelous time together that first evening, except for
one thing: in my nervousness over this first real "date" with
another man since my separation, my face began to flush pro-
fusely, and then my stomach, always a reminder to me of my
sensitive nervous system, began to hurt. As we left the restaurant, John noticed I was uncomfortable and asked whether I
would like to go to his nearby apartment. When we got there, I
felt even worse than before, so I lay down on his daybed and
crumpled into a ball, trying to allay the discomfort I was experiencing. John went to his record player and chose a piece of soft

classical music, then sat down in a rocking chair across the room. There was no talk between us, just the music. I stayed curled up for about a half hour and then took a taxi back to my apartment.

So why was I attracted to John? His intelligence, his sensitivity, his strength, his perceptiveness, and, no doubt, his beautiful hands, which reflected everything I saw in him.

# Dialogue on Appeal

DIANE: It has always struck me as odd that the very things that attract us to another human being can become those things that begin to irritate us. For example, when you and I first began to date, I was so struck by your sense of independence, your sense of freedom, your ability to be by yourself, your passion about your work! I was drawn to those things. Eventually, I think I began to yearn for more of the kind of engagement that I saw early on. But after we married, that same intellectual drive took you outside the marriage instead of drawing you toward the relationship.

JOHN: So an apparent strength turned out to be a weakness? My ability to be on my own and enjoy my independence became a centrifugal force within the relationship.

DIANE: To a certain extent.

JOHN: For my part, I'm struck by the fact that you made such a strong impression on me, both in sexual and intellectual terms. I engaged in no reflection about myself, about you, who we really were, the extent to which we understood each other. I just sailed along, based on these powerful attractions.

Sometimes I think Mother Nature deliberately plays a trick on us . . .

DIANE: [*laughter*]

JOHN: . . . so it can bring men and women together to procreate. It plays upon and, indeed, enhances our ignorance. With knowledge, that procreation might not come about.

DIANE: Maggie Scarf has written that there's something in the genes that attracts people to one another. Something unknown, something unrealized. I do believe that was at work with you and me, because we made an instant connection. Given your inclination to teach, there you were, an attorney at the State Department, here I was, a young woman with no college education. You had gone through college and then law school, but still, within you was that desire to teach, which could have been part of your attraction to me. Certainly part of my attraction to you was to delight in being a pupil.

JOHN: I don't know about the genes. I would hazard it's more a function of the male ego and the Pygmalion complex. For a man to be in a position to be a teacher to someone to whom he is so powerfully drawn sexually simply enhances the attraction. The statue that I as Pygmalion was creating somehow got out of hand.

DIANE: [*laughter*] What does that mean?

JOHN: By virtue of your radio program, you became the learned individual knowledgeable about a lot of issues about which you know more and can teach *me*. But in those early days, being in the position of a Pygmalion was enormously flattering and satisfying. And my subject was so appealing. At one time, I recall seeing you in the lobby of the State Department. They were doing a film about the life of Senator Margaret Chase Smith, and they asked you to walk across the huge lobby as a stand-in for her. There were hundreds of people standing around watching this. I can still vividly recall a beautiful, stunning young woman there in the lobby with all the lights on. The whole incident simply enhanced your sexual appeal.

DIANE: Did you ever talk with any of your male friends about me?

JOHN: I don't recall doing so, and it would have been unlike me. In particular, after I'd finally proposed and given you my grandmother's ring, I didn't tell my friends about our engagement and upcoming wedding. I think this reflected my continuing ambivalence about getting married and sharing my life with someone else. Virtually nothing in my background prepared me for such an existence, and I was therefore both excited and anxious about the prospect.

DIANE: I remember feeling annoyed that you hadn't told any one of your friends. Both of us came together to tell my boss, George Dolgin, about our plans, and he was delighted to have played a role. But I did sense that there was something missing from you: a desire to tell the world you were in love and about to be married! That should've set off warning bells, but if they were there, I chose to ignore them.

JOHN: I do hope you remember, though, how excitedly the two of us together did plan the wedding—every single detail, from the restaurant to the food and flowers. I did want it to be a wonderful occasion.

DIANE: Yes, I certainly do remember every delicious moment.

JOHN: But one of the issues I want to return to is this state of blissful and dangerous attraction. How could we have embarked upon this relationship with greater knowledge about ourselves?

DIANE: Doesn't that go back to, as you said earlier, Mother Nature? Today, young people do seem to take relationships more analytically. They approach them with more caution, taking into account what the other person does, whether this is the person I'd like to spend my *life* with. I think there's a lot more consideration of such matters. Yet look at the divorce rate—almost fifty percent of the marriages that take place today will end in divorce within five years. For all the analysis, preparation, and attention to whatever the problems are, I'm not sure that process really works.

JOHN: So how should young people approach this difficult relationship? To relish the romance, on the one hand, and face the realities on the other?

DIANE: I would urge six months of counseling, with a priest or a therapist, someone who can ferret out the kinds of problems these two people will encounter, instead of just focusing on the bliss. You and I had just one session with the Reverend Duncan Howlett, the Unitarian minister who married us. He asked you then, "How do you feel about marrying a woman who's already failed at marriage once before?" And your response was something like, "Fine."

JOHN: Yes, I had no problem with that. But I'm still trying to grope toward a way in which the romantic illusion will exist but at the same time rest upon some greater degree of self-knowledge, and yet not to the point where the illusion is destroyed. I do think that the illusion is an important part of the commencement, and even the continuation, of a relationship. It's a tricky high-wire act, and there may not be a net below.

DIANE: But what's your reaction to six months of counseling before marriage, talking about the issues you and I have raised—money, profession, family, sociability, for example?

JOHN: Certainly a step in the right direction, but modest by way of preparation.

DIANE: What else can you do?

JOHN: Somehow encourage people to talk about who they really are. That's the key. I thought I knew who I was, and then, in the process of forty or so years of marriage, I learned that, in many ways, I didn't know who I was. Indeed, I turned out to be somewhat different from the person I thought I was.

DIANE: But isn't that the beauty of a relationship, that we become someone new, in the process of living with another human being? In working out those issues, we learn about ourselves. We change some of our ideas. We reflect the other's vision, instead of simply sticking to our own. I've grown, certainly, because of my own efforts, but I've also grown because of my relationship with you, my understanding of life from your perspective, not just mine.

JOHN: I agree. If the relationship continues, it certainly does provide opportunities for learning and for growth. But I'm still fascinated by this threshold question as to how people can get off on a better footing, so that the relationship will continue or at least increase the chances of its continuing. I don't think we yet have in place the key elements of that minimal foundation.

DIANE: You see, I think you're trying to create too *rational* an approach to what is basically a wonderful, *irrational* romance, a coming together. There are no perfect relationships. Every couple I know has gone through some or all of the difficulties you and I have talked about. They may have handled them differently, but they went through them. So trying to anticipate every one of those is impossible. Trying to know oneself completely is a long process.

JOHN: I'm only looking for a matter of degree. But in my case, your beauty and intellectual curiosity did overwhelm me, and thereby undercut the need for a greater understanding of myself—and of you.

# Anger

## John

I grew up intuitively believing that the expression of anger was not only illegitimate but destructive. Like any sensitive child, I was aware of those occasions when my parents were mad at each other. The signs were reasonably clear. They included, for example, curt and chilly exchanges, scowls and other cheerless looks, and a palpable irritability. But on those occasions my parents maintained, however hypocritically, an air of civility. They were thereby able to sustain their anger while still attending to the demands of the household.

The reasons for the anger were beyond my ken, emerging from the mysteries of adult behavior. Over time, I came to realize that my parents, like most adults, had much in common emotionally with children. They simply had cultivated ways of concealing those emotions and contriving a public persona. Nor did I understand what brought these bouts of anger to an end. I was grateful for the return of a modicum of warmth in their relationship, while bracing myself for the next onslaught.

Throughout these episodes, my parents did not articulate but generally observed one cardinal rule: the anger was to remain unexpressed. It was to be contained within the thin skin of civility. The obvious implication was that if the anger were allowed to assume the full force of expression, the skin would burst. The destructive powers of anger would then be unleashed, and our fragile threesome would be gravely harmed.

For the sake of self-protection, I therefore assumed an important responsibility. I became the guardian of the fragile civility, determined not to allow the skin to break. On one occasion when the civility was threatened, I reminded my parents of a popular soap opera of the day, whose title was *Life Can Be Beautiful*. My parents could not help breaking into laughter, and the danger was averted.

Imagine, then, how threatened I was not only by Diane's ability to give vent to anger in loud and expressive terms but her inclination to do so. My paramount reaction was to say as little as possible in reply. I thought that I could thereby salvage, at the very least, some degree of civility. In truth, my attempted silence provoked Diane even more. Moreover, my behavior frustrated any effort to explore the reasons for the anger and ways of dealing with it. It took me years to understand the constructive use of anger, but its expression still frightens me.

A few times, my anger provoked me to destructive acts that left me with quite different feelings. During an angry exchange between Diane and me when we were alone at the dinner table, I seized my dinner plate, lifted it above my head, and then hurled it to the floor, food and all, as hard as I could. I can still relish the enormously satisfying sound of the plate shattering into smithereens. On another occasion, in a fit of rage, I once— but only once—lost control and struck Diane on her right forearm. I derived absolutely *no* satisfaction from this act—only a deep nausea. I remember her words vividly: "Don't you ever dare to strike me again."

# Diane

The extent of anger within me when I reached adulthood was probably more enormous than I had ever realized. Having held it in for so many years, knowing that the expression of anger within my family would not be tolerated, I was probably a volcano waiting to erupt. When my first husband and I became engaged, I broke off the relationship at one point, in the midst of my anxiety over my mother. I couldn't think straight. She was dying, and here I was talking about getting married, which I knew was what she wanted. But somewhere within me that reservoir of anger I'd held on to for so many years was revealing itself, and it came out, in its first expression, at my then fiancé. Ultimately, my anger at the stifling community in which we lived as well as my anger at and disappointment with my husband resulted in divorce.

When John and I first began to date, the divorce was barely behind me. But the anger I'd felt in the marriage was now replaced by an enormous sense of freedom. No longer did I have to fight my way through every single day just to be who I was. Rather, I could work at the State Department and enjoy freedom from fear of judgment and retaliation by the community for expressing my views openly, knowing that this fear had lain beneath the anger and hostility I'd felt in the last days of the earlier marriage.

Later, after my marriage to John, and after the arrival of our son, David, the anger resurfaced. At first, we would simply *talk* about my sadness and loneliness. Later, I realized there was no way I could get John's attention other than to yell, and cry, and, eventually, to scream. My anger at him derived, I believe, from a feeling of being deserted, of being replaced by his passion for work. Why couldn't he cut back on his hours, I demanded. Why couldn't he make time for us? Was his concentration on work a way of avoiding the intimacy I so craved? As the doors slammed and my voice's pitch rose higher and higher, I could see John withdraw into his place of hiding, behind a blank stare I could not penetrate. The more I screamed, the more he withdrew.

As I look back, I reflect on my *in*ability to vent my feelings of anger within my family, especially toward my mother. Perhaps John became a substitute for her: I could yell and scream at him, as I could never have done at her.

It took years and years of therapy for me to understand the roots of my anger, and even more years to realize that the anger had begun to control my life. Even now, at age sixty-five, I find myself sometimes having to repress that urge to holler, and then to find ways to express myself in a reasoned and reasonable manner.

## Dialogue on Anger

JOHN: I must say anger remains a really important issue to me. It goes back to my childhood. Some of my earliest memories relate to episodes when I sensed or knew that my mother and father were mad at each other, for one reason or another. On some of those occasions, they expressed their anger to each other, and I found the expression of anger particularly threatening. I don't have a full understanding as to why I was so affected, but it seemed that by expressing their anger they were, in some significant way, threatening their relationship not only with each other but also with me.

DIANE: What would they get angry about?

JOHN: I don't really recall the issues. We know that theirs was not an easy relationship and there were a lot of mutual disappointments and frustrations. I can't recall a specific episode, but I can recall so vividly a dark cloud that was cast over this little family of three persons when anger was expressed by one or the other. I believed that if anger wasn't expressed, then it didn't exist. And I think that's the notion I carried into our marriage. To express anger is to release all of these sinister, dark forces, whereas if you don't talk about your anger, then the situation remains "normal."

DIANE: So when you and I came into our relationship, one of us was given to express anger, and the other to suppress it. When I would express anger at you, did it scare you?

JOHN: Absolutely. I was seized by fear, because I didn't know what to do, having grown up with this notion that you don't express anger, because if you do, it becomes all too pervasive and all too destructive.

DIANE: So you couldn't fight back, is what you're saying?

JOHN: Exactly right. All I could do was to remain silent and hope and pray that your anger would dissipate as soon as possible and we'd move on. The notion of discussing the anger, the expression of the anger, the reasons for the anger—that seemed like a very hazardous and dangerous thing to do. Far better to treat the episode as if it had never occurred.

DIANE: Whereas in my family, there was hollering, there was yelling, all of it directed at me for some perceived misbehavior, or an attitude that wasn't appreciated, or some chore that had not been completed, which turned into expressions of physical anger on their part toward me. When you and I married, it seemed to me that you tried to *hide* the anger, and pretend it wasn't there; there you were, this stern face, this closed face, icy demeanor. And you wouldn't tell me what was wrong.

JOHN: Well, that was acquired behavior which permitted a little boy, as best he could, to set up a barrier so that the anger wouldn't spill over.

DIANE: Without realizing it, both of us brought our own sense of what anger was, how anger should be dealt with, from our own families into the creation of our own small family, without even being aware that that's what we were doing. We were not thinking about each other, and our own family, as a new entity. What we were doing was reflecting what we had experienced.

JOHN: Playing the old records without dealing with the issues between us. You're absolutely right. But in emotional terms, you were using a nuclear bomb, or threatening to. That was just too much for me to deal with. Therefore, to even begin to get into the area where one could talk with some degree of rationality about the anger was just very difficult for me. The thing that really undid me was the power—and I'm almost prepared to say the *eloquence*—you brought to the expression of anger. It wasn't just a modest amount, it was something *really big.*

DIANE: [*laughter*]

JOHN: Therefore, it redoubled my determination to hunker down and let the storm pass and return to normal as fast as possible.

DIANE: And, of course, that would simply drive my anger further.

JOHN: It's just a classic case of how one's childhood experiences continue into a marriage, and how, certainly in my case, for some years they really crippled my ability to deal with anger and to give it a constructive aspect, which I've learned does exist. Anger doesn't always have to be destructive. It can be the beginning of a constructive dialogue related to the issue in question.

DIANE: Even now, there was a moment here at the farm just the other day when I said something to you about putting something somewhere, and you immediately got very defensive, as though I was somehow expressing anger at you when all I was doing, in fact, was saying something that needed to be said.

JOHN: That's right. It demonstrates my hypersensitivity. I'm very quick to perceive both the existence and the expression of anger. I'll tell you something about this. Let's assume that I'm in the subway, going downtown, and I hear an angry conversation between two total strangers. Do you know that that affects me? I am literally drawn into that, and the fact that they're expressing anger at each other troubles me, even though these are total strangers I'll never see again.

DIANE: But you know, I feel the same way. I can sit in a restaurant and overhear a conversation like that and be frightened for those people, and frightened for myself.

JOHN: And that's exactly where I am. I can recall an occasion in group therapy when one member of the group got mad at another, and the therapist looked at me and said, "John, you have a smile on your face. What's that all about?" And we began talking about it, and I realized that the smile was an effort on my part to make believe the anger wasn't there, or that it would go away. And the smiling, you see, was a way of blunting it and putting it to the side and moving on. The *last* thing that smile implied was an ability or an inclination to deal with the anger.

DIANE: And for me, when I saw that smile—I saw it many, many times as you sat there—it drove me crazy, because it felt as though you were totally ignoring me.

JOHN: I understand that, but the smile was not directed at you. It was directed at the situation, and my desperate need to get away from it as fast as I could. And the smile was one way of masking the problem.

DIANE: The question then becomes, why have things improved? We've both had a lot of therapy. But something has changed within us to help us deal better, more directly, with anger. For instance, I think I don't express my anger the way that I used to. I think I've learned to far, far better control it.

JOHN: Oh, I would agree. I think it's more temperate, and also freer of what I call the "destructive absolutes": the nevers, the evers, the alwayses. When people get mad I think they reach out for the universal, all-encompassing words.

DIANE: We've been talking about our own anger. I'm wondering to what extent we've passed our attitudes on to our own children. We raised two wonderful kids, but at times they saw the anger, the hostility, the hatred being expressed. They heard the slammed doors. They heard the long silences. So they in turn will have to deal with their internal models of anger, just as you and I did.

JOHN: Do you think they're in a better position to deal with anger than we were?

DIANE: In my own case, my parents were gone, and I didn't have an opportunity to engage with them as an adult, and perhaps have a chance to move on from their model. David and Jennie have both had that chance. In your case, your father died when he was just seventy-two. Your mother died in 1990, and her hold on you, as far as anger was concerned, continued until she died.

JOHN: Do you think I was better able to deal with anger after her death?

DIANE: I definitely feel that her death freed you in some ways to allow yourself to express your own anger. She was one who could never, ever express anger. She would act it out in strange ways. But once she was gone, without your even realizing it, you found a new freedom within yourself to express your anger toward me—which was constructive. Finally.

JOHN: You've drawn a good distinction between, on the one hand, how I react to another person's anger—yours, in many cases—but also how I would express my own anger. I've been talking for the most part about my reactions to the expression of anger by others. I've found it a *little* easier to express my own anger, although its negative implications, its threatening aspects, are still there. But I think I've made some progress in viewing both sides of anger.

DIANE: And I think that's one of the most important and positive elements of a long-term relationship. We do learn, we do grow, we do change, because we're living so intimately with someone else. If I were living alone, I wouldn't have to absorb or reflect someone else's anger. I've heard people in group therapy say to me, "Your anger scares me." And I would hear *your* voice in that. Even though you had never actually used those words, I would understand what was happening to you through them. And so I think I've become able to express my anger in quieter, more constructive ways. At the office there used to be times when I'd really blow my lid! I rarely do that now, and I don't think I do that with you, either.

JOHN: Well, of course, now we're touching upon a really important point, which is how, in the maturing process, we learn to deal with greater skill with so many of the emotions that beset normal human beings, anger certainly being one. For me, anger has been a significant test of my own maturation. And the distance I've come, however great or small, in dealing with anger is certainly part of the growth that I've experienced.

DIANE: I feel the same way about myself.

# Family

## John

In recent years, I have come to realize that, as a single child, I grew up without a sense of family. This may seem odd, since the apparent signs of a family were present: after all, I lived together with my father and mother, each of whom unquestionably loved me, albeit in different ways. In turn, my father and mother assumed the roles of spouse and parent. As a threesome, we celebrated such familial events as Christmas and birthdays. Together we spent time at the beach on Long Island and frequented authentic Chinese restaurants in lower Manhattan.

What, then, was missing? I would say a devotion to one trilateral relationship, as opposed to a series of bilateral relationships. The absence of such a devotion sprang from the estrangement between my father and mother. It remains a mystery to me why they married in the first place. Although they could be quite charming and outgoing with others, each was powerfully drawn to a solitary life. As a result, I recall very few instances when, by a word or gesture, they communicated their love for each other. I think a kind of love was there, but it was rarely manifested.

As I grew up, therefore, I had two separate links—one with my father and one with my mother. But the triangle was rarely if ever closed, because my father and mother never established the link between themselves. Indeed, their relationship—such as it was—was grounded primarily in their attachment to me. This was the one powerful interest they had in common. But this placed upon me—or caused me to assume—the responsibility of keeping the threesome together. This is a burden that should not be placed upon any child.

Accordingly, without a parental model to draw upon, I had to create my own sense of family. At the time, I couldn't have expressed this thought so clearly, but as our son, David, arrived, and then our daughter, Jennifer, I haltingly began to understand the dynamic interrelationships among four human beings who are in the process of living together. Such interrelationships are made all the more complex because over our—at times, strenuous—resistance, they are constantly evolving. I sensed that Diane, for her part, brought a strong sense of family, both immediate and extended, to our marriage. I learned from her, in particular, the great value of having the four of us celebrate the events of the calendar year, including the Christian holidays, together.

# Diane

Having been raised within a family I didn't understand and could never trust, I created within myself an image of the kind of family I wanted. The family of my dreams consisted of my adoring husband as a loving and caring father, myself as a warm, protective, and unselfish mother, with two beautiful and well-behaved children. Where did that dream come from? How can I know? Magazines, movies, radio, and, later, television programs and ads. Somehow, I believed that this fantasy could be my reality if I worked hard enough to achieve it. It was absolutely contrary to what I had experienced in my family of origin, where I felt neither safe nor loved, and where, as a child, I believed I was the bane of my mother's existence.

Perhaps many of us assume that by leaving our family of origin with a mate, we can make up for what was lost—or never found—in our own childhood. I believed that the love John and I shared in those exciting days of courtship and early months of marriage would help us create the "ideal" family relationship, where all was understood, where loving-kindness was always present, where arguments never occurred, either between the two of us or between us and our children. And I *always* assumed that if there did happen to be disagreements between one of us and a child, the other parent would surely step in to reinforce the position of his or her partner. Never in my wildest dreams could I imagine one parent disagreeing with the other over the disciplining of a child. All I had ever seen or known was my father supporting my mother in her strict attitudes, insisting that I eat certain foods (whether I liked them or not), present myself in certain ways (always neat and clean, without wrinkles in my dresses, with hair combed and braided), and strictly obey the rules my mother set down.

Imagine, then, how stunned I was when, after I had lovingly sewn and smocked dresses by hand for Jennie as a toddler, she announced at age four that she did not want to wear dresses anymore (the word "tomboy" fits well here). Not even to church! I was aghast, and argued my position loudly with her. To my utter frustration, John took her side, one of many occasions where he supported the children rather than express his support of me. He argued that if she felt more comfortable in corduroy pants, that's what she should be allowed to wear. Of course, at the same time I took his statements as a further reminder of the fact that he didn't care about church and would just as soon the children not go at all. Arguments about clothing quickly turned into larger issues, my sense of "appropriateness" versus his. I felt like the outcast, with two children and one adult lining up on the other side, and I was furious.

The same tensions arose when I'd serve scrambled eggs for breakfast. Jennie hated scrambled eggs, and I insisted she eat scrambled eggs. Why? Most likely because I had been forced to eat a boiled egg each morning and had internalized the requirement. The awful irony was that I had hated those boiled eggs so much I had somehow managed to camouflage an egg cup to make it *look* as if I had eaten the egg. I would then take the egg and get rid of the uneaten evidence in the woods behind my family's house. No one had supported *me* in my hatred of those eggs, so how was it that our children could find support from John to prevent their having to eat foods they didn't like?

I tell that story because it strikes me as a vivid example of how each of us believes we are acting as an independent being, free of the impositions placed upon us by our parents. Unless we work at it, investigate it, and struggle with it, we will likely never be free. Maggie Scarf eloquently makes this point in her remarkable book *Intimate Partners,* saying that we can *"see the ways in which aspects of [our] intimate world have been picked up from the past generation and are being reenacted and repeated in the present one."* That is, of course, unless we become consciously aware that we are assuming those roles for ourselves. But back at that early point in our marriage, it never occurred to me that this was what I was doing. I was behaving in a way that was familiar to me, however distasteful my own childhood experience had been. I was acting out the role of my parents, insisting that food be consumed for its nutritional value, taste and preference be damned.

When John stepped in to say that surely there must be alternatives to scrambled eggs to produce a nutritious breakfast, I felt I was once again being cast as the family villain.

So here we were, two people who had come from extraordinarily different backgrounds, with totally different parenting styles as our models, and acting out what we knew because of our own parents' behavior toward us as individual children. John felt he was absolutely correct in defending his children's rights to make their own decisions, even if defending them meant opposing me. That was what his family of origin allowed—even expected—him to do. I, on the other hand, believed children should adhere to my directions without question. I was the person in charge. John was barely there. How dare he come home and overturn rules I had laid down? How dare he assume the role of "good guy" as soon as he walked in the door? How dare he disagree with me, in calling into question the only style of parenting I knew? And how dare he, after all, not act as my father did, by agreeing with every action my mother took? It felt like total betrayal, and led us both, out of our mutual frustration, to engage in ugly screaming scenes.

# Dialogue on Family

JOHN: In talking about family, I find myself surprised—surprised that we created a family as the kids were growing up, and, maybe more importantly, surprised that we have sustained the family even as David and Jennie have gone their separate ways with their own families.

DIANE: Why are you surprised?

JOHN: I think it goes back to the basic fact that I never had a conception of a truly organic family. I thought that one got married, had children, and the mere coexistence of parents and children ipso facto created a family. And I think you taught me . . . you know, we do learn things in marriage . . .

DIANE: [*laughter*]

JOHN: . . . I think you taught me that if a genuine family is to be created, with a genuine set of reciprocal relationships, it takes work, it takes thought, it takes a constant determination to keep this often fragile entity called a family together.

DIANE: As I watch Jennie and her husband, Russell, deal with our grandson, Benjamin, I see a true partnership between them. I see Russell doing so much—bathing Benjamin, changing Benjamin, playing with him. I see the two of them in true partnership with that child as an infant. I missed your participation with the children when they were young. As they got older, you were out in the street playing soccer, baseball, with both of them. But when they were younger, you didn't seem to be an organic part of their lives.

JOHN: I think that's true. Looking back, I can see that as a young man in his late twenties, early thirties, I was overwhelmed by all the demanding roles I was expected to play: successful lawyer, affectionate husband, caring father. In some ways, it was just too much. I didn't feel I could handle all of it. The route that was easiest for me was to work and work and work, and to give short shrift to the other aspects of our marriage.

DIANE: Why do you think you became monomaniacal about your work?

JOHN: Because it allowed me to succeed intellectually and earn the regard of civil servants whom I greatly admired. Then, too, at the time our culture celebrated the work ethic. My addiction to work was therefore within—not outside—the values of the day. I was doing what was expected of me. So I felt trapped between society's demand that I work *more* and your insistence that I work *less*.

DIANE: Did those people at work in some sense provide you with a semblance of family?

JOHN: Yes, I think that's right. But I do want to stress this key point for me: if you don't grow up with the conception of a true family, if you don't have that in mind—and I think you did—it's very difficult to enter into marriage and then creatively begin to put together an effective family. I think that was probably true of me until David and Jennie reached early adolescence. Then I could relate to them on a number of levels.

DIANE: Well, from your own adolescence. You saw David loving baseball, loving soccer and football, Jennie doing the same things, and you really could relate to them on that athletic basis.

JOHN: And I was also able to do so on the academic front, discussing various topics, showing a genuine interest in what they were learning, helping them from one course to another.

DIANE: So you entered the family on a physical and intellectual basis, but not on an emotional basis when they were quite young. That's not to take away from the fact that I can still see you bouncing Jennie and David on your knee and reading nursery rhymes and other stories, and they adored you. There's no question but that they adored you.

JOHN: But again, I want to go back to the idea of family as a complex set of numerous reciprocal relations. I really took quite a while—some years—to reach an understanding of how that works, and how it's to be maintained. I can think of times when you and Jennie weren't talking, for example, and I mediated between the two of you.

DIANE: Comfortable role for you, to be mediator.

JOHN: Absolutely, because that was the model my parents gave me. But I also began to get a sense of what is constantly required, day in, day out. I don't want to make this sound dreary, but it does take a lot of attention and work to sustain the family, once created. There are always centrifugal forces at work, and I'm impressed that, in recent years, I think the two of us have consciously worked at maintaining the family. I think we've succeeded to date, and I think we will succeed. Both our children feel themselves to be part of the larger family in a genuine sense.

DIANE: I think we both had to work at that, too, recognizing that, as they grew up, our children weren't going to be perfect imitations of us. They weren't going to reflect every single one of our expectations or our beliefs. That has been interesting for me to watch—both the similarities and the differences.

For us to acknowledge that we need to back off in some cases, to just let them develop in their own ways, as opposed to trying to impose our systems on them.

JOHN: You've just anticipated a point I was about to make, which is that there is a constant tension. On the one hand, you want to maintain the contacts by phone and by writing, gifts and so forth, but at the same time you don't want to try to get them too close. You want to give them, and acknowledge, their right to lead their own lives. There's a lot of subtle give-and-take, to keep them within the larger family and at the same time not deny them the freedom they should have.

DIANE: Do you think there was any training we might have had beforehand that would've enabled us to anticipate what these challenges were going to be? I cannot believe that you and I are the only two people in the world who've had these kinds of shifts and passages and difficulties. Just take adolescence. My dealing with David or Jennie through their adolescence challenged me in *my* adolescence. My adolescence had not yet been played out, and here I was reacting to their adolescence through my own, instead of through an adult vision. It was very frustrating, to them and to me.

JOHN: You ask whether there might have been some training available. Isn't that one of the fundamental problems we're dealing with in each of these topics—the lack of preparation, the lack of anticipation, the stumbling from one point to another? Yes, I think we could have benefited from some kind of training or instruction. But I frankly don't know where we would have turned to get it, since we didn't get it from our parents. Isn't it one of the massive paradoxes of our culture that all these demands are placed upon us as husband, wife, father, mother, with no preparation? It's almost as though we're expected to stumble and stumble, and somehow in the process keep this fragile entity called a family together.

DIANE: Of course, all I had in training for motherhood were memories of my own mother and Dr. Spock. That was the only book I turned to at the time, though there were other books available. Now there are volumes on every stage, from infancy through adolescence and into the early twenties.

JOHN: Maybe there are too many such books today. The field is overcrowded with manuals of one kind or another. To get back to the fundamentals and use them as creatively as possible—that's the trick, it seems to me. And not spend all your time as a would-be parent reading tome after tome.

DIANE: But the problem is that most of us come to parenthood without the maturity to be good parents. So you've got to have some assistance unless you've come from a perfect home, a perfect background, which I just don't believe exist.

JOHN: I fully agree. You know, I think so far Jennie and Russell are doing a fine job in raising Benjamin, but in a way these early years are the easiest. We'll have to see what happens as Benjamin grows up and is beset by all the pressures of this world.

DIANE: Of course, as far as Benjamin and David and Nancy's son, Alex, are concerned, you and I are now moving into the role of grandparents, which extends the family even further. It becomes yet another new family experience.

JOHN: Yes, and that's why I have come to understand the need to establish and to maintain a family. I think that we try to achieve both largely by staying in touch with our children and now grandchildren. So it's very much an ongoing process.

DIANE: It's a lifetime of learning.

JOHN: As is marriage itself. But again, I don't want to make this sound like a grim enterprise that you embark upon. There's fun, there's pleasure, there's love.

# Making Love

## John

The first time Diane and I made love was an ecstatic experience that is still fresh in my mind. On a warm fall afternoon, the whole world seemed to devolve into one union of one couple in one bed. All demands and responsibilities were suspended for several magical hours. That afternoon seemed to presage many more of an equally carefree and ardent mood.

The mundane realities of marriage made it all too difficult to perpetuate that illusion. Those realities came to take many forms, to my surprise and chagrin. For example, making love competed for discretionary time with other activities. I found it difficult to plan the event in advance, since that would rob it of the desired spontaneity. Moreover, it seemed crass to attempt to prioritize making love against the demands of raising two children, preparing meals, maintaining a house, and the like. All too often, therefore, I let it go, nagged by my sense of Diane's disappointment.

But setting aside the competition for time, making love often became a psychological weapon, wielded in marital skirmishes and even war. Withholding it was a form of retaliation for the infliction of real or imagined wounds. Restoring it after a period of destructive silence was an awkward means of expressing regret. Demanding it as a form of release disregarded Diane's feelings and wishes.

In short, making love became problematic. At times its presence offered a means of reconciliation, when other avenues were cut off. At other times, its absence exacerbated the tensions between us. Yet throughout our marriage, making love has somehow retained its fire.

# Diane

I feel very shy as I write this section. It is, I would think, to any couple *the* most private and intimate area of a relationship. Yet I do believe there are some aspects of the sexual interaction I can speak about, without going beyond what I would consider appropriate boundaries of expression.

First, I felt exactly as John did the first time we made love. It was a perfectly gorgeous day, sun shining, breeze blowing through the windows of his apartment. It was a moment we both cherish and recall happily, signaling, for me, a new way to embrace the sexual encounter, for the first time realizing how beautiful it could be. I loved John's emotional gentleness as well as his physical strength, his understanding of my mood, and his caring words. It was a very promising beginning to a mutually satisfying relationship.

The two of us are quite certain that I became pregnant on our wedding night, because David Bartram Rehm was born just

seven days short of nine months after we celebrated our marriage. During the period of anticipation of a new arrival, we
continued to enjoy our lovemaking, taking greater and greater
care as the time of delivery approached. But our passion for each
other, and our playfulness with each other during that first nine
months, was joyous.

After David Bartram Rehm arrived, a number of factors
began to affect our desire and intensity. First, fatigue. It hits all
parents. After the birth comes the recovery period, which in
those days allowed me to remain in the hospital for five days, a
luxury that young women do not enjoy today. Then, the shock
of going home, just the two of you, with this beautiful baby boy.
But relishing the joy doesn't last very long, because immediately
the middle-of-the-night feedings begin. Quite frequently John
would get up with me to sit and talk while I fed David. While I
treasure the memory of those moments, they were followed by
bleary-eyed mornings, each of us struggling to find the energy it
takes to care for a new human being and to face another day.
Then, with John at the office working from eight in the morning until at least seven or eight in the evening, I would try my
best to live up to my own expectations of myself as a perfect,
nurturing, caring new mother. I don't think I'm alone as I recall
those early days. Many of my good friends have told me they
experienced the same kind of utterly endless fatigue, trying to
do it all.

What was left in the way of energy in those early months of
parenthood was minimal. I had little, if any, interest in lovemaking, and John seemed to feel the same way. He didn't
approach me, and I didn't approach him. It was as if we had
gotten *out of the habit* of pursuing our sexual relationship. We

thought so much about how to deal with the everyday practicalities of life with a new baby that we had no time or inclination to think about ourselves, our wants, our desires, or why we weren't resuming the simple and loving but provocative gestures that newly married couples engage in.

A number of therapists I have spoken with have indicated that the relationship between two people changes after the first child is born. It is as if the couple has entered an altered terrain, necessitating learning a new geography, and it takes time to sort through it.

In our case, the arrival of the much beloved child coincided with the intensification of John's career, and is the important second factor that I believe affected our early sexual lives together. One can argue, of course, that John may have, consciously or otherwise, been *comfortable* with the fact that his work was so incredibly demanding. Perhaps this allowed him a reason to distance himself from the demands and responsibilities that a wife and new baby boy present.

Finally, once the fatigue of the early months of child-rearing had passed, it took some time to readjust to even a minimal level of lovemaking. We had been changed by the experience of having a child.

# Dialogue on Making Love

JOHN: For many years and into the present, I have carried with me what I call the romantic illusion with respect to making love. What do I mean by that? I mean the notion that making love occupies a special but separate area in a marriage, that it somehow transcends what's going on in the relationship, its problems and difficulties. It's like a little island. Not only does it remove you from the prevailing problems, but—and this is the key to the romantic illusion—it will do away with them. It will do away with them during intercourse itself, but also beyond. If you can get to that privileged, lovely little island, all will be made good.

DIANE: I'm glad you started that way, because I have such a different feeling. As a woman, for me the sexual encounter is very much an extension of the emotional encounter. Time and time again, when we have been distant or isolated from each other, you have approached me sexually as a way to move beyond the problem. But I am still in the problem and therefore can't move that quickly from the emotional feelings I'm experiencing, turn them off, and move toward becoming a sexual partner.

JOHN: I understand that very well. Therefore I've found myself needing to provide a realistic approach to making love, complemented, perhaps, by what I call the romantic illusion. In that realistic area, I know of instances where I tried to use making love as a way of seeking forgiveness, of trying to reconnect with you. At times when I have done so, you've made it clear by word or gesture that you weren't interested. However valid your excuse, I've typically been caught up in two related emotions. The first is the bitter feeling of rejection and, in turn, isolation. Emerging from this is the strong desire to retaliate by withholding my own sexual participation the next time *you* show interest. But by doing so I risk further sexual estrangement, in which case my strategy boomerangs.

DIANE: Though sex probably is one of the first attractions that people feel toward each other, it's interesting how complicated it becomes, how enmeshed in all of the day-to-day problems—the fatigue of raising children, the intellectual attachment to what's happening at the office or outside the home. It becomes a much more complicated relationship than one can imagine after those first beautiful encounters, which often take place with the idea of producing a child. I agree with you about the romanticizing of making love. I, as a woman, have certainly romanticized the sexual act. Yet at the same time, I've felt too often that *because* it's been used as a weapon to separate or distance us, to try then to use it in the opposite way, to try to *connect* by it, is equally difficult. You and I have had long periods when we did not connect, because we weren't on the same emotional and sexual plane. We were working individually and separately, and it was hard to find a meeting place.

JOHN: More recently I think I've tried to achieve a balance between the romantic illusion and the realistic understanding of the sexual act in the context of a relationship. But I don't want to make this sound bleak, because I think you'll agree that there have been instances where making love has at least *assisted* in restoring a degree of connection and intimacy. So the notion that it shouldn't be used for some other end beyond itself—I don't think that's correct. On the other hand, I also think that, at times, I've expected too much of making love, that it would in some curious way not only suppress but maybe eliminate the existing problems. So I quite agree with you—it becomes complex. And that complexity at times is daunting and can in itself reduce the urge to make love. I can remember a time when I went off to South Africa—and we were barely speaking. I wrote you a note, later, saying that I almost asked the taxicab to turn around as I was leaving the house for the airport, because I knew how emotionally distant you were from me at that time. I was afraid that you wouldn't be there when I came back. But on I went to South Africa. In that note I said that each time you and I talked on the phone from Johannesburg I became increasingly fearful that I had indeed "lost" you. I said the tone of your voice over the telephone was really frightening to me because it seemed so distant. We had suffered, before I left, a long period of noncommunication, part of our pattern through a lifetime of living together. When I did come home, I did so very tentatively. I came home emotionally, as well as physically, needy.

DIANE: And it was that emotional aspect of you that I could see and respond to, and so when you approached me physically, I felt not only your physical need but your emotional hunger. That was what allowed me to respond to you.

JOHN: Another aspect of this topic that I want to talk about briefly is what I call the "absolutist" approach, and this may in part be due to the difference in physiology between men and women. If I'm going to make love, it's got to be the "big bang," if you will. I don't know where I got that notion, but it's still with me, and at times has inhibited my reaching out to you sexually, Diane, because I wasn't quite ready, for a variety of reasons—physical, psychological, what have you—for the "big bang." Therefore better to put it off, build up the expectation, so that it would be more likely to be the "big bang," as opposed to what I think is a more realistic and healthy approach, which is to recognize that there are degrees of making love, both in physical and emotional terms. It can be moderate, it doesn't always have to reach a stunning climax; there are ways of being together sexually that don't always involve the "big bang." I've had to work hard at that, and I think it's something that you understand better than I.

DIANE: There's another thing I want to say to you, and that is that, throughout our marriage, in many ways and not just in the sexual encounter, you do have this tendency to postpone pleasure.

JOHN: So that it will be all the greater.

DIANE: Perhaps.

JOHN: That's my illusion.

DIANE: That's your illusion. That's part of the romantic illusion, and it does seem to me that it takes away from the acting out of the natural urge. If you keep postponing, you don't act on the urge. Now, obviously, people have to restrain themselves from acting on the urge every single time it occurs.

JOHN: But you see, in my view, there's a correlation between the two: that is to say, the longer the wait, the greater the pleasure.

DIANE: Well, baloney. Of course, as a woman, I don't have that expectation that I must always *achieve* physically. Achieving is not what it's all about for me. You've often said women have it so much easier than men. I'm not sure I agree with that. But I do know that for me, the sexual encounter is as much about holding one another closely as it is about achieving what you call the "big bang." That hugging, the smell, the touching of the flesh, the warmth of the breath, all of that is so powerful to me as a woman.

JOHN: But I think I'm typical of most men in this regard. If I could wave a magic wand and relieve men of at least one burden that they carry through life, I would relieve them of this need that we feel in ourselves to achieve the "big bang" in the fullest sense of the word, with each act of making love, so that we could return to a more modulated approach and recognize, as you've just said, Diane, that hugging can be just as meaningful, indeed perhaps as powerful, as the full climax. Not easy for men to understand in our culture, which does, I think, in a kind of macho way, expect the big bang each time.

DIANE: As we age—you've heard that expression, "Use it or lose it"—you're now seventy-one years old, I'm sixty-five, I would expect our sexual lives to go on forever, in some way, but not necessarily in the same way it occurred when I was twenty-three and you were twenty-nine.

JOHN: But are you suggesting that sexual intercourse will last forever? I somehow doubt that.

DIANE: In some form, I do believe it will last forever. The adventure, in whatever form it may or may not take.

JOHN: I would certainly expect and hope that the sexual encounter, in at least some sense, will endure and continue. But we'll have to confront certain physiological realities over time.

DIANE: Well, we'll see. [*Laughter from both John and Diane*]

# Solitude

## John

The little boy is absorbed in pushing the toy train across the kitchen's hilly cobblestones. Deep in his bed, the adolescent relishes the colors of his feverish dreams. The young man opens the door to his apartment, happily anticipating its emptiness. The older man sets off on a long walk owing no allegiance to anyone—however temporarily.

These are vignettes of some of my happy experiences, and they all manifestly involve solitary pleasures. From time to time, the company of others brings on a deep thirst to be alone. Assuaging that thirst is like taking a long draft of cool spring water. From the time of my boyhood, I have been strongly drawn to the figure of Robinson Crusoe. Thrown back upon himself after a shipwreck, he achieves both security and pleasure in his solitude.

As far as I can tell, this part of my character springs from both parental and environmental influences. My father and mother both favored being not lonely but alone. They had the intellectual resources to avoid being lonely, although my mother desired the companionship of others more than my father. Yet I remember how consistently each sought out his or her private pleasures. That was the model I was given and absorbed.

The model was enhanced by the fact that I spent my first two or three years with few playmates. During that time, while my father worked for the Paris *Herald Tribune,* we rented a little apartment in Paris during the winter and a small farmhouse outside Paris in the summer. As a result, I can recall only one playmate, whose name was Michel, and even he was available only some of the time. Nor do I have any memory of my mother playing with me. Like Robinson Crusoe, therefore, I had to create my pleasures in solitude.

If for me solitude is rich in happy connotations, for Diane the word evokes pain, in particular bringing to mind the many times she was punished by being confined to her room. Thus, what was a haven for me was a prison for her.

That difference in our histories certainly led to difficulties and misunderstandings between us. I found myself using that very desire for solitude as yet another weapon against Diane, a way of distancing myself from her, even though I knew full well the anxiety I was thereby causing her.

Over the years, however, two complementary things have happened. On the one hand, after long periods of struggle, I have come to realize the joys of sharing more openly with Diane, offering up not only my daily activities but the feelings I experienced. She and I have learned to be together in new ways, to listen more carefully to each other's words—the implications we make and the inferences we draw. At the same time, Diane has discovered her own joy in being by herself, in writing in her sewing room overlooking the garden, working among the flowers, or reading a book.

# Diane

Today has been a glorious day for me. I am alone. I have been by myself all day, in the privacy of our home, with all the windows wide open, feeling a soft breeze blow into my sewing room. I have worked in the garden. I have paused to breathe, closed my eyes to relax, and have not uttered a single word to anyone today. I am truly ecstatic.

What an incredible difference this is from those early years of our marriage, when I was anxious and fearful each time John left the house, whether for work or on an errand. What has happened to change me and my outlook? Maybe it has been just the "growing up" that each of us has had to do, shedding the past and freeing ourselves from childhood images.

When I was a young girl, I was very active in all kinds of sports, including tennis, basketball, kickball, and baseball. I was constantly playing with other people, enjoying the cheering, the laughter, the competitiveness, and the encouragement of teammates. All of this took place at our neighborhood playground in Washington, D.C., Twin Oaks, at Fourteenth and Taylor Streets, NW. As a youngster, I would run up to the playground as soon as school was over; this became my daily ritual. Freedom! Companionship! Playfulness! They all awaited me at Twin Oaks.

Of course, my mother realized how much all of this meant to me. So to punish me for some infraction, I was forbidden to leave the house. I can remember looking out the window of the upstairs bedroom I shared with my sister, watching my friends play outside, knowing I couldn't be with them or share in their fun. There were times when that punishment would last for weeks, and along with the pain of being confined came the fear of my mother's wrath. She wouldn't talk with me during those periods, and I didn't dare try to cross her path. Late in the afternoon, when she'd call me downstairs for dinner, she would place the meal on the table and leave the kitchen before I entered. The whole experience of her punishment left me with a terror of being left alone.

Imagine, now, two people who have come together because of mutual attraction, similar interests, shared ideals, and what they each termed "love." But we had such extraordinarily different outlooks on solitude, and neither of us talked openly about it—what it meant to us, why it was important, or what the experience felt like. John viewed his solitude as "a draft of water." I associated solitude with punishment. How was it that two people married to each other wouldn't have discussed that idea, that need, *before* marriage, rather than after? And why has it taken nearly forty years for us to adjust to, accept, and even relish our differences?

## Dialogue on Solitude

JOHN: Solitude is an issue on which you and I have actually drawn closer, namely, whether we are or aren't comfortable with being alone, derive pleasure from being alone, and do significant things while being alone.

DIANE: I think when we were first married it was very hard for me to be alone, and I needed to spend as much time with you as possible. Certainly, before David was born, we did spend a lot of time together, taking long walks and having long talks over dinner, and I thought that was going to continue. I never thought that our marriage would include long stretches of isolation, or aloneness. And yet the very marriage proposal came only after three weeks of your aloneness, after I had walked out, after we had broken up, after you had proposed and then said you had "forgotten" that you had proposed. I was so outraged I went down to Virginia to stay with a friend. We didn't talk for weeks.

JOHN: I think I was trying to confront, perhaps not in a very effective way, the whole notion of living with someone else for many, many years. That was so contrary to my upbringing, to a model that I had conceived in my mind, namely, of an individual who spends most of his time alone, in what I regard as a productive solitude. But marriage entailed a constant cohabitation, and that was very hard for me to accept. Suddenly I was confronted with a serious loss of freedom, loss of independence.

DIANE: How different do you think you are, even acknowledging your background, even acknowledging what some would call your *extreme* feelings about solitude? How different do you think you are from other men of your own generation, or young men today?

JOHN: In terms of solitude, I think I'm distinctly different. In terms of a reluctance to make a commitment, which I think is a different issue, there I think I probably stand with the majority of men. But I think most men, when they're not in the company of wives or girlfriends, like to be with each other, at a local bar, or hunting, or watching a ball game. With the exception of watching ball games with our son, that has never interested me, and never will. The idea of sitting in a bar talking over a beer is alien to me. So in terms of my "thirst" for solitude, I think I'm somewhat extreme.

DIANE: So that living in that household with a wife and a first child, it became harder and harder for you, except when you were in the privacy of your own office, to find the kind of solitude you were looking for.

JOHN: Yes, and the problem was enhanced by the fact that during the day I was constantly with my colleagues and other professionals. I enjoyed working with them immensely, but that created an even greater need for me to be apart and by myself. Which meant taking time away from being with you and the children and participating in family life. The tension became even stronger, ironically, the harder I worked.

DIANE: It sounds to me as though you were very much focused on your own needs.

JOHN: Unquestionably. Growing up as a single child, doted upon by mother and father, I could do no wrong. That created a certain selfishness in me: that is, my desires and needs came first. For me to enter into a family life, for which I had no model in terms of my own parents, presented a lot of problems for me.

DIANE: Is this, in fact, a warning to young people who may be considering having only one child, that the child may grow up too much by him- or herself, that the child is given more attention than a child in a larger family, and spends too much time alone?

JOHN: I don't think that being a single child, by itself, creates this model I'm talking about. I can think of single children who are very socially inclined, and happy to be with people. In my case, the parental model, plus my circumstances, drove me into solitude, and for some reason or other, I was able to take advantage of solitude. For others, it might have been a hardship. For me, it offered an area where I could be myself, be true to myself, and, like Robinson Crusoe, be thrown back upon myself.

DIANE: We started out this conversation by saying we've grown closer to each other in this respect. So much so, in fact, that now on Saturday mornings when you leave the house to go grocery shopping, I find myself tempted to run through the house naked, hollering, "Yippee, yippee, yippee!" I cannot imagine a more dramatic change than that feeling of being utterly *joyous* at having time by myself. Also, I've sometimes believed that had you *not* been as you were—and still are, to a certain extent—I wouldn't have been thrust back on myself to create my own life, my own interests, such as playing the piano, sewing, cooking, all very solitary experiences. I literally threw myself into them.

JOHN: So you're saying that my behavior, paradoxically, encouraged your cultivation of solitude, even though it was something you hated as a child.

DIANE: And beyond that, if you had been the all-doting husband, if you had been that protector, that comforter, that all-present male who was going to save me, who was going to make my life absolutely wonderful—if you had been that, perhaps I would never have pursued my own career. I would never have looked for my own interests outside the home.

JOHN: To get back to the notion that we've come closer on this issue of solitude—solitude versus social behavior—I still dread small talk. I feel awkward engaging in small talk. . . .

DIANE: And yet you're so good at it.

JOHN: Deep down, though, it's still difficult for me. But I think you've taught me that at times one can construe small talk as a sign of affection and respect. So that it's not so much what the small talk is about, but that it's a vehicle whereby people, somewhat obliquely, perhaps, do express fondness, affection, and the like. I've been able to see that a little more clearly, as we go out to dinner or to a movie with friends. So I don't cling to the specific subject of the small talk, because, by and large, that's going to bore or irritate me. But I'd like to find more people who get excited, the way I do, about Chinese portraiture of the Ch'ing dynasty, for example, or a single piece of Hindu sculpture.

DIANE: Even I can't get as excited as you do, because I'm not as informed as you are on that kind of topic. Maybe you're expecting too much and might have to change *your* own approach to being a social human being. . . .

JOHN: [*laughter*] Well, I don't think I'll change my approach very much. But I'm not talking about an intellectual level of interest—I don't really look for that. I just look for an expression of enthusiasm.

DIANE: And interest.

JOHN: And you've given me that. You've done tours with me when I've been practicing my presentations, for example, and you've evinced such enthusiasm! That's what I look for.

DIANE: The other thing I've found with regard to small talk and being able to close the gap not only between strangers but between friends is to ask questions. You've been able to do that more, and found yourself somewhat surprised at the kind of information you elicit. And that, in turn, stimulates conversation between you and someone you wouldn't have expected to be of interest to you.

JOHN: I accept that. Another way to put it is that one can find in small talk things of value: comments, perceptions, and the like. But it's still hard. Given the fact that we came to this issue of solitude in our marriage from two such different points of view, what could we have done to ease the problem? How could we have begun to close the gap so that I would feel that I had a right to a certain degree of solitude, and yet, within bounds, you could accept it and not become frustrated or angry?

DIANE: Once again, if you and I had been able to sit down and talk about this, either before we were married or during the early months of marriage! If you had been able to say to me: "I know that you need a lot of socializing, and you enjoy the company of others, and I need a certain amount of solitude. How can we work this out?" Your needs could have been satisfied, and mine, too. Instead, what we seemed to have done was to go to war over the issue. I interpreted your need for solitude not as a need for yourself but as a need to *reject* me. That was the difference.

JOHN: You've raised the fundamental question, which runs through so many of our conversations, which is: Why do couples go to war instead of negotiating peace? What can be done to promote peace, as opposed to waging war? That's what it often comes down to. Each person is stubborn, believes he or she is right, and is unwilling to yield. But I think this kind of behavior comes out of—one of my favorite themes— our ignorance of ourselves. I think you and I see ourselves more clearly now. Before you can negotiate peace, you've got to have some understanding of who you are. You may be trying to work toward peace but not know how to do it. Somehow, to fall back on confrontation and war seems easier and more satisfying.

DIANE: I agree. If we could only learn to be more open in our feelings—they don't have to be fully thought through or fully articulated—and to express them. I'm feeling lonely. You're feeling the need for solitude.

JOHN: But that demands a maturity that I would hazard to say most couples don't have in the early years of their marriage.

DIANE: Unless, as our children both did, they marry later in life, or, as some other couples do, live together and don't marry. They may be more open to the expression of feelings. You have a hard time with that.

JOHN: I have a distinctly hard time with that. I was emotionally immature when we married. You mentioned the need to be open, to hear the other. You know, it takes a lot of self-confidence as well as maturity, a comfortable feeling about oneself, to be able to open up and share feelings. That doesn't come easily. It takes time. And so we're leaving our poor young couple, newly married, struggling to find each other and themselves. It's a tough path.

DIANE: One area of assistance that's open to many couples who do marry within the Episcopal church and many other denominations today is a period of premarital counseling. That's now a requirement of many priests and bishops. Six to eight sessions of premarital counseling, on a once- or twice-a-week basis, whether within a religious setting or otherwise, might have saved us a lot of grief. We might have uncovered some of those up-to-then relatively hidden characteristics each of us had, and been able to see them as part of the person each of us was about to wed. I wish we had found a way to undergo that kind of open exploration, with the guidance of a counselor who had the maturity to understand and point out the problems we were heading into.

# Money

## John

For the most part, I don't recall my parents arguing over how money should be spent in managing the household. During the depression years, my father managed to remain employed in a series of low-paying jobs. Moreover, we obtained some monetary assistance on my mother's side. But from what I overheard, I gleaned that there was little to argue about.

My father's attitude toward money was quite simple. If you have it, spend it; if you don't, manage as best you can without it. My mother's approach was the contrary. Spend as little as possible now in order to ensure that you will have some later. A collision of views was averted by the fact that my mother held the purse strings. How that came about I do not know, but my father seemed content with that arrangement.

They both shared an antimaterialism. Neither longed for goods such as clothes, furniture, cars, or jewelry. They both enjoyed dressing well on special occasions, but drew upon a modest wardrobe. Through their eyes, I regarded poverty as a sign of social superiority. It promoted the kind of simplification that Thoreau extolled in *Walden*. Moreover, poverty placed us in the grand intellectual tradition of disdaining material wealth.

As a result, I don't recall many serious disputes over money, with one recurrent exception. Even during the lean years, my father saw to it that we ate well. This meant porterhouse steaks, roasts of pork and lamb, and such seafood as clams, oysters, and lobsters. My mother regarded such foods as unnecessary luxuries, and would have settled for more modest meals featuring fresh fruits and vegetables. In this arena, however, my father had his way, despite my mother's grumblings.

In handling money, I adopted both my parents' antimaterialism and my mother's frugality. In particular, I distilled four injunctions from their experience. Deem *things* of little value. Live within your means. Save regularly. And avoid debt, if at all possible. As a result, I have been drawn to few possessions, except for books, recordings, and a few paintings. The vast majority of belongings should be primarily utilitarian, with style being a secondary consideration. I still resist the notion of acquiring an item—like a piece of furniture—primarily for aesthetic reasons.

Before marriage, I was comfortable with my four-point creed. It suited my lifestyle and encouraged me to spend money wisely. I was able, for example, to pay off my law school loan within a year or so after graduation. I paid cash for the first car I purchased. And I had the resources to finance the drilling of a badly needed well on my father's farm.

Diane, however, brought to our marriage a distinctly different attitude toward money. Diane has never been a spendthrift, and in the early years of our marriage we had just enough money to cover basic expenses, so there was little room for dispute. Then, as our discretionary income increased, our true colors showed. For example, Diane insisted the time had come to refurbish the interior of our home, including painting, plastering, redoing floors, and purchasing new furniture. To accomplish this would require taking out a second mortgage on our home. The fear of additional debt overwhelmed me. I resisted for a number of years but finally relented. The issue became the subject of many long and frustrating arguments between us, however, until she convinced me that the work on the interior was just as important as keeping the exterior of the house in good condition. These differences continue to surface from time to time, but we've learned to negotiate and to work earnestly to understand the other's position.

In the early years of our marriage, the issue of who would control the money arose between us. In my family, it was my mother who wrote the checks, paid the bills, and saved what she could. My father did not seem to object. His very passivity may have strengthened my resolve to be in charge of the money, both before and after our marriage. Even though Diane and I had a joint checking account, I wrote all the checks until one day Diane demanded that she write the checks covering her own needs. I can still recall how shaken and enraged I was by her demand. I can remember attempting to punish her by withdrawing from her for some time. Her presumptuousness seemed to undermine my preeminence as head of the household, including breadwinner and controller. It took me some time to relent and grudgingly accept Diane in this new role.

# Diane

Dimes and quarters. Nickels and pennies. That was usually the extent of my dealings with money as a child. A dollar bill rarely crossed my palm. I knew our family was not rich, but neither did I feel poor. There was always good food in the house (thanks to my father's grocery store), and my mother always seemed to have money for the "extras" she needed, though she cautioned me not to tell my father about the purchase of items like Elizabeth Arden powder, perfume, or face cream. I think she would save her money carefully for those purchases, then give me the money and send me downtown to Hecht's department store to purchase them for her.

My father suffered a heart attack when I was twelve, and our circumstances changed. For the first time in her life, my mother had to go to work. Her extraordinary skill with needle and thread led her to take a job at the Hecht Company in their monogram department, where she worked five days a week. I recall the sadness I began to feel when she was no longer at home when I returned from school. It meant, for the first time, a darkened house, without the smells or sounds of her presence. It was also then that I became aware of conversations about money, and a sense that we had become weakened as a family because my father could no longer work. His stock market holdings had lost substantial ground, and my mother now had to leave the house each day for a job. It was an uncomfortable situation, and one that became the undercurrent of our family life from that time on.

I began to earn a weekly allowance for doing daily chores

assigned to me. These included emptying trash cans, dusting, mopping, ironing, and starting dinner. At sixteen, I was told to find a job to supplement the family's income, as well as to provide for my own clothing purchases. I went to work as a file clerk at the Hecht Company, working after school each Wednesday afternoon and all day Saturday.

As a result, I learned the meaning and power of money at an early age. I knew I wanted to be secure in the sense of having "enough" money, whatever that meant. In my first marriage, I didn't experience that luxury. My husband and I lived from week to week and paycheck to paycheck, concentrating on paying for food, clothing, and just the basics of living. There was no thought of setting aside money for buying a home, for example. We lived in a pleasant apartment, but the rent plus food and other necessities took every penny of our combined income. I hated the feeling of being limited by a lack of money, perhaps because I had internalized too much of my mother's feelings of frustration.

When John and I first married, those limitations were, again, very much in play. His salary was small by today's standards, about thirteen thousand dollars a year as an attorney for the State Department. Yet he believed strongly in the need to purchase a home as quickly as possible, a dream I'd long held, and we managed to do it, with the help of his mother and my former boss and his wife, George and Lee Dolgin. From that time on, money was extremely tight. To make sure that we could meet the monthly mortgage and car payments, each week we would draw up a list of necessities, decide how much we could afford to spend, then shorten the list by half. But at least it felt as though we were moving forward. Indeed, at a cost of ten dollars per month, we bought a sewing machine, so that I could begin to make my own clothes as well as clothing for David and, later, Jennie.

On balance, I believe John and I are in agreement about how to use our money. Of course, our circumstances have changed considerably over these past forty-two years, and we now have much greater financial comfort. However, John remains more conservative than I in his outlook. He's more of a saver than I am, although I've never been a spendthrift. When, after years of living in our home, I wanted to give the insides a complete face-lift, he balked. And balked. And balked. I think it took about four or five years of nagging before he finally agreed to move forward with redecorating the entire house, which truly needed it.

By that time I had begun to earn a small income, so I believed I deserved a say in how our money was spent. That is what the issue finally came down to: Should I, as the minor earner, have as large a say as he, the major earner? Or should that even be a factor? After all, we were partners in marriage, weren't we? Sure, he was the one out there earning the bulk of the money to support us. But I had been taking care of the home and our children. Didn't that merit acknowledgment? Those responsibilities didn't earn me money, but they were what freed John to concentrate on his career. It was a matter of fairness. We should both have an equal say in how the money was spent. But it sure didn't feel that way.

# Dialogue on Money

JOHN: The topic is money, not in the sense of something to be budgeted but rather in the sense of the emotions we bring to the idea of money. Emotions that we may not be in touch with. In my case, I think I tried to shield from you, in the early years of our marriage, my essential anxiety about money: the feeling that money is always to some extent hazardous, that it may not be there for everything we want—maybe not even for basic necessities. That's certainly a carryover from the fact that I was raised toward the end of the depression, and while I don't recall my parents talking about it much, there's no question but that I picked up my mother's concern about money and its availability.

DIANE: I certainly have a tendency to be willing to spend money. From the time I was sixteen, as you know, I went to work. I saved up enough money during that time to buy my first bedroom furniture, which was really something for me. I knew I could buy it "on time" and put a certain amount of money down, then pay an amount each month. So I learned, by the time I was seventeen or eighteen, that you could budget for something, and it could be yours. I sensed, whether you told me so or not, that you felt, Oh my gosh, can we afford this?—a certain fear, except when it came to buying a house. You felt we should purchase a home immediately because it would give us an instant foundation.

JOHN: You're right about that, and looking back, I'm a little surprised that I was prepared to make what was a gamble at the time. From our earliest years together, we agreed to set aside enough money for the kids' college education, about which we felt very strongly. But as we approach a potential purchase, I think you and I differ in a fundamental respect. My inclination is always to put off a purchase, so that the money will be there for some future purpose.

DIANE and JOHN: [*laughter*]

JOHN: Your inclination, within bounds, is, Oh, let's buy it, because we have enough money. I immediately react by asking whether there's really a valid reason for making the purchase and so reducing the amount of money we have.

DIANE: Which is why I would sooner go shopping without you than with you. I shop with an eye for what I believe we need. Therefore I'll go through the store and see things I hadn't thought of and realize, Oh my gosh, we need that. And I'll get it right then and there, because my point of view has always been, if you need it, buy it when you see it; if you come back later, that perfect thing that you want may be gone. Your attitude is always, Well, now let's think about this and whether we *really* need it.

JOHN: That's right, and I have to confess that's still the case. When you go into a store and see something you like in the way of a dress, say, and you buy it, in the back of my mind is the feeling, Well, she *wants* the dress and she'll justify its need later.

DIANE: [*laughter*]

JOHN: Which is another way of saying the need is not really that conspicuous, but you'll buy the dress anyway, and if I press you, you'll come up with a reason that will justify its need, when in fact it was simply desirable.

DIANE: Money gets into clothing, gets into purchases for the home, gets into the very elements of our makeup. You spent your high school years, for example, wearing modest clothing, and you had a group of friends who did the same thing. Now what I think that did was to implant within you the idea that all you needed are the most modest kinds of clothing. And then you transferred that attitude to our house itself. Do we really need this new chair? Do we really need this coat of paint? This whole approach to money began to display itself in so many different ways.

JOHN: Dealing with me is tough because, as I've been thinking about it, this emotional underlay of anxiety is accompanied by a strong antimaterialism. I'm basically not in favor of buying *things*. Sure, necessities, but beyond that I'd probably stop if I had my way. So that, Diane, you were encountering these two strong strains that were within me. The anxiety on the one hand—better not to spend now, and save for another day—and also this strong antipathy to things and the material articles of life.

DIANE: Now take the redoing of the house, which was a huge issue for us. You kept saying, "No, it doesn't need redoing, it can wait." And granted, it required taking out a second mortgage on the house. When it was finished, and when I had come through absolutely on budget for everything involved, you loved it.

JOHN: Oh, I quite agree. But we're dealing with both the rational and the irrational. Rationally, I did love it, and you did a fine job having the house refurbished. But that didn't eliminate my initial anxiety, and probably an enduring anxiety about paying off the second mortgage.

DIANE: I'm struck by the fact that Maxine Thornton Denham,

one of our therapists, used to say to us that sex and money are two big issues in any marriage. We've talked about sex, making love, and the anxiety there. Do you agree with her that those two issues are big ones that any marriage has to face?

JOHN: I probably do, and of the two, I would say money is the more difficult. Assuming there is an attraction between two people, as there certainly has been between you and me, at least one element of sex is a genuine, immediate pleasure. Money, as I look at it, draws on some of our deepest feelings, some of the essential aspects of our personalities. I think therefore it remains an issue. What we would hope for is to find ways of managing the issue so it doesn't get out of hand and lead to major confrontations.

DIANE: I think in this forty-second year of our marriage, we may have reached that point. As an example, I very much want to create an addition to our home. We've talked about this for a number of years, and at first you said to me, flatly, "No, this is silly, this is ridiculous. You and I are in this house alone—we don't *need* an addition to the house." Instead of arguing with you constantly about that, what I've done is let some time pass, and let some attitude sink in, some suggestion about what the house would look like. Then you came to me finally and said, "You know, I'm not prepared to do this now, but let's see how the economy goes in the next year or two. Then let's talk about it." To me, that seemed far more reasonable and rational, and I was willing to accept it.

JOHN: And I think I was encouraged by your acceptance of it. It suggested that you aren't, as I would put it, irrationally determined to go ahead and put on the addition, come what may, whatever the state of the economy, whatever the state of our retirement fund. So I think one can say there's been some movement on both sides.

DIANE: I really think there has. I've learned what your sensitivities are. For example, if we go into a store to buy you a specific item—say, a jacket you've expressed the need for—I'm now not foolish enough to try to get into an argument with you about buying a pair of shoes for yourself, in addition to the jacket.

JOHN: Well, that's right. It really used to irk me a lot, because I'd say I need a shirt, or whatever, and you have a very good eye about these things. We'd go in to buy a shirt, and before I know it, we're talking about a jacket, a tie, and shoes.

DIANE: [*laughter*]

JOHN: And immediately my anxiety and antimaterialism would raise their ugly heads, and I'd say to myself, Here we go again. This is not rational purchasing. This is spur-of-the-moment irrational purchasing. And there we were, at loggerheads.

DIANE: That's interesting that you call it "spur-of-the-moment irrational purchasing." I would say, Now that John is here in the department store, I have him to try on such things—which you *obviously* needed.

JOHN: But I felt at that point that I was being used, that you had finagled me into the store to buy something that, admittedly, I'd said I needed. And then, suddenly, I'm deluged by all these other items. . . .

DIANE: But the fact of the matter is—

JOHN: So you took advantage of me. . . .

DIANE and JOHN: [*laughter*]

JOHN: That's what it comes down to.

DIANE: And the fact of the matter is, I don't do that anymore.

JOHN: Much less, but I think it did feed what is probably a prevalent male feeling, which is that when women go into a store, objective need goes out the window and it's all impulse buying.

DIANE: It's *not* all impulse buying. . . .

JOHN: And they do it to relieve their own anxieties of one kind or another. We all know about these great purchasing binges designed to ease some kind of neurotic need.

DIANE: [*laughter*] Do you think *I* go on great big neurotic purchasing binges?

JOHN: No, but I would say that there are occasions when you've brought home more clothes than you needed to.

DIANE: Well, those are my passions.

JOHN: Exactly. And the passion is irrational. That's my thesis. Men and women have to learn that they have very different approaches to the purchase of things.

DIANE: But don't forget that passion does feed the soul.

JOHN: Yes, but passion can also destroy the soul.

DIANE: In *my* case, passion feeds the soul.

# Profession

## John

Our culture has demanded that I—like so many others—become an adult by learning multiple roles. Above all others, these include being a spouse, parent, and professional. Getting a grip on any one of these roles is hard enough. My upbringing afforded me little preparation for taking on these daunting responsibilities. Nor did it give me even a hint of the further challenge—that is, not only the mastery but the integration of all three roles.

As far as being a spouse and parent goes, I gave these two roles little thought before marriage. But three impressions in particular rose in my consciousness. First, my parents were of little help, since they rarely shared with me their thoughts about performing these roles. Second, love was a sufficient foundation for becoming a successful spouse and parent. Third, the process of doing so would take care of itself and not require conscious thought and overt action.

I could not have been more wrong. For the first several years of our marriage, I focused compulsively upon my professional career and neglected my other roles. Far from achieving any degree of integration, I didn't even achieve minimal success in these two familial roles. It fell to Diane to salvage the little she could, spending most of her time alone with two small children.

Even today, I'm struck by the fierceness of my dedication to my career as a young lawyer in the government. What caused such fierceness?

It was certainly not a desire for money, since government salaries were perennially modest. I think it was a combination of ideology and the recognition I received. Over a period of about thirteen years, I worked at an increasingly senior level on the U.S. foreign aid and trade expansion programs, in which I believed wholeheartedly. I felt that I was making a contribution to the cause of economic integration and reduced conflict among the countries of the world.

Moreover, as a lawyer, I found myself working closely with Foreign Service officers whom I came to admire greatly. They combined intelligence, expertise, and, above all, a deep commitment to their jobs. In turn, they gave me respect, as well as encouragement and even affection. I felt needed and supported by outstanding professionals promoting both our national and international interests. It was all very heady for a lawyer who was not yet thirty.

For some years, I paid a heavy price as an inadequate spouse and distant father. I knew full well that my wife was not only lonely but angry. I also knew that I was missing significant experiences with my children. Though they were undemanding, I knew that they were saddened by my absences. When I was at home, gone were the recognition and satisfaction I received from the professionals with whom I worked. Gone was the support for my efforts. At home, I was just another human being, struggling against Diane's anger and hostility. During that time, my work was an addiction, and the gratification it gave me largely blinded me to the harm I was inflicting on my family.

Indeed, a vicious cycle set in. The more time I spent at the office, the more angry and frustrated Diane became, and the sadder my children. In turn, I retreated all the more into my work in a vain effort to minimize the clashes with my family. After all, I could understand and direct my work, whereas I had little comprehension of—much less control over—what was happening at home.

In fact, I had mixed feelings about Diane's behavior. On the one hand, I felt she was wrong in berating me for working so hard, instead of being supportive and sympathetic like a good wife. On the other hand, I acknowledged to myself—but certainly not to her—that I was allowing my work to dominate our lives to an unhealthy degree. The tension between those two feelings served to exacerbate the problem.

My behavior as a young man was without doubt reprehensible. But after all these years, I still sympathize with that young man's plight. He was the sole breadwinner, anxious to move ahead for the benefit of his wife and children. At the same time, he was ill equipped to meet the competing demands of career and family. It would be years before he—prodded by Diane and supported by therapy—was able to understand, and, to a degree, integrate all three roles.

# Diane

Never in the world did I dream of having what is called a "profession." It was simply not part of my vocabulary, or, strangely, even my dreams. I grew up accepting the idea that my "title," if you will, would be, first, wife, then mother. To my mind, that vision was totally satisfactory.

What I had not counted on were the changes going on in and around me: the ferment of the sixties and seventies with regard to women and independence; the explosion of ideas that led to questions about self and marriage; and the freedom to express myself, to react in my own ways to art, to music, to politics and literature. Up until that point, I had unquestioningly and gratefully accepted John's beliefs. But then, as a result of conversations with individuals and groups of female friends, I began to consider my life and its possibilities in a new way.

Yet even then, venturing out of the house to find a profession seemed far-fetched. Instead, I gave myself over to various volunteer organizations, working with other women in the church, organizing dinners, heading up adult learning programs, serving on the church governing body, and broadening my circle of acquaintances. After taking a course at a local university called "New Horizons for Women," I happened to speak with a woman who had just begun volunteer work at a radio station here in Washington. That idea held great appeal for me, and I asked whether more volunteer help might be needed. She inquired, and through that chance encounter, my "professional" life began.

I have now been the host of a nationally and internationally broadcast radio program for the past twenty-two years. It has changed my life, and our lives, profoundly, and given me a sense of accomplishment I wouldn't have imagined for myself. But its impact on our marriage has been both positive and negative.

In the early stages of my development as a radio broadcaster, John was enormously pleased for me and frequently proclaimed his pride to our children, to his colleagues, and to our friends. He bragged about me a lot. He talked about the kinds of issues I was dealing with, the people I had on the program, and the number of times he heard the show in taxicabs.

But slowly, the more well known I became, the greater the unease I sensed in him. I began to feel some resentment, particularly over our attendance at events to which I had been the person invited, rather than he. When we went to such functions, more people knew me and wanted to talk with me than with him. When we walked into a grocery store or stood in line at the movies, strangers would come up to express their appreciation for the program, and I could sense that John was put off. After years of having his professional status be the focus of our relationship, the tide was turning.

Picture a scale with a single brick on one side, weighing 165 pounds. The scale remains lopsided for at least fifteen years. Then a small stone is added to the other side, at first weighing perhaps as little as twenty pounds. But slowly the weight of the stone increases while the brick remains steady, and finally there is a move toward equilibrium. As those two weights, representing our professional lives, evened out as a result of my totally unexpected move from the background into the foreground, we had to struggle to try to find a new way to be together in our marriage.

And now, with John's retirement after forty-five years of practicing law, we enter yet another new stage together. He's found numerous activities in which to be involved and from which he takes great pleasure. I maintain my professional career, which continues to interest and even excite me. I'm not ready to let go yet, and it will be interesting to assess the impact on our marriage of our two now different lifestyles.

# Dialogue on Profession

JOHN: The topic of "profession" gives me a chance to advance one of my pet theories. If one were to have asked me, "What was your profession?" I would have said immediately, Practicing law. But of course that's profoundly wrong. In fact, I had and have at least three professions, or what should be considered to be professions, all demanding knowledge, discipline, and experience. In my case, those two additional professions were husbanding—being a husband to you, Diane—and parenting—being a father to David and Jennie. Of course, our culture doesn't regard husbanding and parenting as legitimate professions, no more than it does mothering. It just occurred to me: suppose Harvard College should announce that part of its undergraduate curriculum would include Parenting 101. It would be laughed at all over the planet.

DIANE: Well, society seems to say parenting is so important, and we must appreciate the role of the parent, yet there's no effective recognition of parenthood.

JOHN: There's a vast degree of hypocrisy here. People from the president on down talk about being a good parent as well as being a good spouse. But in terms of marshaling the available resources, so little is done in a structured way that would begin to give young people some preliminary sense of what faces them, what the demands will be, and how they can cope with them.

DIANE: You're now getting into the demands of parenthood. But in terms of a professional life, I've always felt that part of your sadness, anger, and depression was that, in fact, you chose the wrong profession for yourself. Back in college, you were a Greek and Latin major, and at first you considered teaching. Then, as you explained it to me, you believed that teaching would be too insulated a profession. You shocked your parents, and even yourself, by opting for law school. You hated law school, every aspect of it. You then went to a law firm on Wall Street, and you left that for government service in Washington. You loved those thirteen years of government service. But the practice of law in the private sector was never something that really made you happy.

JOHN: I would agree, but I'm trying to assess the impact my profession—the law—had on our marriage. Do you think we would have had an easier marriage if I'd chosen a different profession?

DIANE: Well, if you had chosen a different profession, we would probably have never met, so that's a moot point. But what I'm saying is that you are basically a scholar. You love to study, you love to learn. And I think that part of your own frustration was the fact that you chose to practice law. I had the luxury of choosing or falling into a profession I absolutely adored.

JOHN: But looking back, the happiest years of my life as a lawyer, namely, my years in government, were probably the most difficult years of our marriage. It was because I thoroughly enjoyed what I was doing in government and believed so strongly in the programs I was working on that I took away so much time from being husband and father.

DIANE: I fully agree. You were happiest in your professional life practicing law in government, but you were also engaged in the practice of making *policy* during those years. I also think you're right that those were the most difficult years for us because you were so totally involved. Once you moved into private practice and had to worry about fees, billable hours, and clients—all that seemed contrary to what you, John Rehm, were comfortable with. I think the practice of law became almost distasteful to you. There was no more of the kind of fun you experienced in the government. Do you think that's fair?

JOHN: Yes, but let's return to the central issue. How does a young family cope with having either one or both spouses so dedicated to their profession that some kind of deprivation is going to be inflicted upon the family because they will be spending so much time at the office?

DIANE: It's never perfect, I'll grant you that. There are certain sacrifices that have to be made. But they can be eased if there's an acknowledgment that, even with this ongoing tension and pressure, home life is as important as work life. I realize the pressures are always there. I think of Jennie and her husband, Russell, two physicians, who've now said they're going to take one day off per week so that they can be with their children and have more time as a family. I think—I hope—young people are acknowledging the problem, and moving more in that direction.

JOHN: Greater accommodations are being made today. I look back on the year 1962, in particular, when I literally spent almost every day of the entire year working on what became the Trade Expansion Act of 1962, which was President Kennedy's major piece of legislation in the international field. If I was to remain thoroughly involved in that significant project, I didn't have much choice but to spend virtually all my time at the office and then come back on weekends exhausted, when all I could do was to sleep. How could we have coped with that any better?

DIANE: You made the decision that you would give everything you had to that project.

JOHN: And that was expected of me at the time.

DIANE: That was expected of you at the time. But later, do you remember what Governor Herter said to you when he was the U.S. Special Trade Representative and you were his general counsel?

JOHN: He said family must come first, and job second. I understood that, but rightly or wrongly, I felt powerless. If I was to be a key player in the enactment of the Trade Expansion Act of 1962, then I couldn't afford to set aside time for the family. Diane, you don't know how trapped I felt, but that was the only way I could see to go. I so believed in the project, and the project would after all be temporary, only a year long, and after that I imagined we could return to a more normal and more sane lifestyle.

DIANE: But it never happened.

JOHN: So what is this poor young man to do? I feel so sorry for him, because he's so trapped. He's doing his best—*trying* to do his best—to meet all of these competing needs and conflicting demands. It's really tough.

DIANE: I understand that it's tough, and I understand that, looking back, what you're really saying is, "I feel sorry for the memory of myself in that situation. I feel sad for myself because I didn't know how to cope." What about me? How sad do you feel for me that I went through those years, from the time those kids were little until their adolescence, practically alone? You can't convince me, John Rehm, that there couldn't have been a way for you to be a forerunner and to say, "I need to be with my family this weekend, and therefore that's what I'm going to do." I'm so impressed with young men and women who do that today. I also recognize that the first man who did that in your law firm was ridiculed by some. He said, "I have a brand-new child. I'm only going to work part-time." And your partners were aghast. There's a new culture at work, and I thank heaven for it.

JOHN: Do you recall your encounter with Abe Chayes, the legal adviser of the State Department?

DIANE: At one point you had promised to devote the entire weekend to our family. We had plans to go off on a picnic, to do some sightseeing with the children, and then a problem arose at the State Department.

JOHN: We were working on a set of regulations, which never came into being, to control shipping to and from Cuba.

DIANE: So I'm making all these plans, and all of a sudden you come home on a Thursday night and you say to me, "Abe Chayes wants me to work this weekend." And I say, "Well, *you* promised us that you would *not* work this weekend, and I believe you should abide by your promise." At which point you went back sheepishly into the office on Friday and told Abe Chayes how upset I was. He picks up the phone and calls me. He says, "Diane, this is Abe Chayes. I *really* need John this weekend." And I say, "Well, Abe, *I* really need John this weekend." And he said, "OK, look, I promise you that if you give me John this weekend, you can have him for the next *two* weekends." He made that promise, and he kept it.

JOHN: I was in his office at the time he made the call. He thought it was going to be a piece of cake. Of course, I couldn't hear what you were saying, but I could see he had an easy look on his face at first, and then it became more tense and more surprised. I don't think he had ever faced this kind of vehemence from the wife of one of his lawyers.

JOHN and DIANE: [*laughter*]

DIANE: Sweetheart, it was tough, and I understand that, but I felt you gave your entire emotional and physical being to that office.

JOHN: I suppose we could ask whether I really did need to devote all of my time so monomaniacally to this project. Was I getting out of it something I badly needed, in spite of the harm it was doing to our relationship?

DIANE: In my work, the balance between professional and home life was uppermost. I began doing some runway modeling, and then volunteer work at various organizations, and ultimately the volunteer work at WAMU, which thrilled and enthralled me. It was all I could think about, I was so excited about the possibility of doing some work through a medium I adored. But I had to arrange my volunteer life, which became my work life, around the needs of the family, and that was what I did. I was both mother and, early on, a professional volunteer.

JOHN: But wouldn't you agree you had greater opportunity than

I did to shape your schedule to begin to accommodate your increasingly professional life to your home life? I think you had greater latitude to do that than I did.

DIANE: Absolutely. By the time I took the full-time job at WAMU, as host of the morning program *Kaleidoscope,* Jennie had just gone off to boarding school and David was in Paris. I didn't feel constrained at that point. But in recent years I've experienced some of the same professional pressures you endured: the greater the success of *The Diane Rehm Show,* the fewer hours seem available for family life. So, ironically, I am somewhat in the position you were in.

JOHN: Which better enables me to help you safeguard time for us.

# Religion

## John

From childhood up to the time of my marriage, I probably attended church only a very few times. When I did, my attendance was a matter of social obligation, with no religious overtones whatsoever. Indeed, those few occasions served only to sharpen my disdain for institutional religion.

My father and mother were brought up in the Lutheran and Episcopal traditions, respectively. By their account, they experienced, and were repelled by, the horrors of orthodoxy. Accordingly, following my birth they readily agreed that I would be spared such contamination as baptism, confirmation, and communion. As an adult, I would then be free to make a mature and unbiased decision about such matters. As I grew up, therefore, the Bible in our house was at best a work of literature.

Once we decided to marry, Diane expressed her desire for a church wedding. She had grown up an active participant in a variety of church-related activities. As an agnostic, I was opposed to a Christian ceremony, since I viewed Jesus as no more than a shadowy historical figure. I wasn't prepared, however, to deny the existence of any kind of God. As a result, Diane and I were able to settle on a brief service in a Unitarian church.

After David and Jennifer were born, Diane very much wanted them to be baptized in her Syrian Orthodox church. This presented a serious problem for me, since I couldn't accept any of the beliefs underlying baptism. I finally relented for two reasons. First, Diane felt so strongly. Second, as infants, they could not grasp, and therefore could not be affected by, the Christian dogma. They too, I reasoned, could make up their own minds when the time came.

Primarily for the sake of the children, the four of us began attending a liberal Episcopal church committed to social causes. Consistent with my muddled monotheism, I did not recite the Nicene Creed or other Christian passages, nor did I participate in Holy Communion. I was more comfortable with the Old than the New Testament. Diane, meanwhile, threw herself into a number of projects and became an influential parishioner. The marked difference between Diane's activism and my passivity created a tension between us. This tension grew as our involvement in the church spread to social functions among the parishioners. I fitfully resented the time we devoted to so many aspects of church life. I felt that Diane demeaned herself and, by extension, our family, by her participation in the life of at best a silly, and at worst a destructive, institution. In my eyes, it stood for hypocritical self-righteousness and did not deserve support.

In June 1979 I experienced an overwhelming seizure by, and understanding of, Christ. The conversion was profound and led to my baptism later that year. It also prompted me to obtain a master of theological studies degree in 1990. I think that, for some time, Diane did not know what to make of my conversion.

Although we were now both Christians, the radical nature of my faith, in contrast to Diane's more conventional belief, was at times divisive. In particular, as an insider I was now even more critical of the institutional church and its corruption of Christ's teachings.

Our spiritual journeys began and indeed progressed in distinctly different ways. We still part company over theological issues, since Diane is more of a conventional theist and I am in the mystical tradition. The former assumes a caring God, while the latter, to my mind, speaks of a more abstract power. Yet today we together gratefully observe the essential Christian ceremonies. These include the celebration of holy days, like Christmas and Easter, the singing of hymns, the participation in the Holy Eucharist, and the offering of prayers.

# Diane

My faith in God has been a part of me ever since I can remember. There has never been a time of doubting or questioning. There has never been a time of anger or blaming. I have simply accepted God as a central part of me, a voice, a shape, a spirit to whom I give thanks each and every day, and from whom I ask help and guidance and care for those I love, and for those around the world. My prayers are an integral part of my daily existence, as I walk through our garden, as I walk the distance between my office and the studio at WAMU, as I gaze at our children and grandchildren, and as I read the newspapers. There are always reasons to pray, and they are a central part of who I am.

I was saddened by John's lack of interest in and even hostility toward the notion of having a specific religious affiliation early on in our marriage. It was difficult to understand why he seemed to have such antipathy toward something that was so deeply embedded in my heart and in my culture. But realizing that he had no interest and did not particularly favor my moving toward any church affiliation, I did not wish to create a problem between us. However, when David and then Jennie were born, there was no doubt in my mind that they should be baptized. I could not relent, even though I knew John would not fully participate in the ceremony or accept the ritual behind it. In fact, John was intellectually drawn to each baptism, but had no feeling about the idea of blessing an infant as a child of God.

Once the children began school in the mid-sixties, I made the acquaintance of a number of parents. One couple in particular talked to us about their Episcopal church in Washington, St. Patrick's. Its rector, they informed us, was deeply involved in the civil rights movement, to which they were not particularly sympathetic. However, the parish was thriving, with many people, old and young, drawn by the influence of the Reverend Thomas Bowers and his wonderful wife, Margaret. The two were quite a pair, warm and welcoming, drawing parishioners into what felt like an enormous family with a primary goal: desegregating the parish, the Church, and the country.

Slowly, we became involved in church activities, attending not only services but social functions organized around the parish. These were days of energy and excitement for me, getting out of the house, meeting new people, attending retreats, and pursuing more deeply my examination of our marriage.

Getting to know other couples, watching their interactions, being part of their social circle, seeing a different way of being in a marriage—all of this came to me through those early years of church affiliation. The ideas I heard and the actions I observed began to change me and my outlook on our marriage, our life together, and the prospects or possibilities for my own future.

# Dialogue on Religion

DIANE: Religion is one of those areas we didn't really talk about at all, except that I knew, vaguely, that you were not particularly interested in participating in church activities. Initially, for me, it was a kind of relief, because I had come out of a marriage where the church was the center and the focus of the community. To that extent, I was relieved not to be involved with any church affiliation.

JOHN: Looking back on our marriage, I recognize that during the first twenty years or so, religion was a divisive factor in our relationship. Whether you were going to church regularly or not, you were clearly a Christian in the full sense of the word. You accepted the Nicene Creed. It was meaningful to you. Until my conversion experience in 1979, you can say I was atheist or agnostic. I certainly had no use whatsoever for the institution of the Christian church.

DIANE: But this is the case in many couples' marriages, where one may be particularly filled with the idea of God and religion and the other is not. What you're saying is that you found yourself deeply resentful.

JOHN: Yes. It was really your decision to begin to take the kids to church, and I didn't object particularly. I figured they could handle that on their own. But your involvement in the church grew, and you became more active by serving on committees and the like. That left me nowhere. I didn't believe in what was said during the church service. I didn't participate in its functions. At one point I was asked to serve on the vestry, until the rector found out I hadn't even been baptized. [*laughter*] So, until my conversion experience, I was vexed and annoyed by the degree of your participation and activity in the church.

DIANE: But was it my social involvement or was it my emotional involvement that vexed and annoyed you? I think this was something that really bothered you, that became far more symbolic to you, far more emblematic of our division. You almost wanted to keep me from the social, emotional, and intellectual involvement of the church.

JOHN: I think that's fairly put. The church had an emotional significance for you that it didn't have for me. I think I was somewhat envious of your faith, even though I didn't put too much stock in it.

DIANE: *Envious* of my faith?

JOHN: Yes. The sense that you had of God, of a divinity. It's not easy to be a struggling atheist.

DIANE: I think the other element that got to you relates to the subject of friendship. It was out of that religious group that came some of my earliest and deepest friendships within the marriage. Friendships I could rely on, people I could turn to. And that's where religion spilled over into an emotional freedom from the marriage that I found myself experiencing. I found myself battling against you as I went. You not only didn't believe in God, you didn't believe in the Nicene

Creed, you didn't care to go to church, but you also didn't want to have me involved socially, or to bring you along into that social group.

JOHN: Because, you see, you were an active participant in an institution that I respected not at all. In my eyes, you were *tainted* by that participation. Ideally, in those days, if I could have I would have kept you from this degree of participation, so that you wouldn't be swallowed up in the social activities of the church.

DIANE: But what does "swallowed up" mean? Does that mean I'm taken away from you in the process?

JOHN: I saw it then as a kind of impairment of your integrity. To be so associated with this worthless institution demeaned you in my eyes.

DIANE: Wow, that's quite a statement! I've never heard that before. To be *tainted* in your eyes strikes me as really quite dramatic.

JOHN: I mean it, because, for me, the institution was so hypocritical.

DIANE: It still is. It always has been.

JOHN: That's right. But in those days I think I felt particularly strongly about that aspect of the church. So I would've kept you away from that involvement, but it was obvious that I couldn't. So I somewhat passively and unhappily and—

DIANE: "Grudgingly" is the word.

JOHN: Yes, "grudgingly" is the word. . . . I went along with your activity. I figured the kids wouldn't be too harmed by their superficial exposure to this tradition.

DIANE: Your grudgingness, your feeling that I was somehow

tainted, your intellectual and emotional antipathy toward the church say to me more about *you* than about me. They say to me that you were struggling within yourself to find a way toward God and, at the same time, wrestling against it.

JOHN: I think that's unquestionably true. And even though I would have branded myself as atheist or agnostic, I was aware of certain strains within me that were reaching out for something. It was an internal struggle that was manifested externally in these ways.

DIANE: Scoop, here is an area where I felt you were mean-spirited. You did not behave charitably. You attempted to foist your own ideas on me, without the generosity or maturity to simply acknowledge that we were different in that regard. We were simply different. We could've spent years and years exploring this before we were married, and then we might never have gotten married if we had talked about all this in the first place. But why were you so mean to me about this?

JOHN: Because I felt you were drawing me into an excessive degree of activity, like going off on vestry retreats. I did go with you—

DIANE: And you had such powerful experiences. I think of Manresa, the very first retreat we went to, and how powerfully drawn you felt yourself to be.

JOHN: But still resisting at the same time.

DIANE: Do you remember we saw an eclipse of the sun from the hill at Manresa?

JOHN: Of course I do. But "mean" is a strong word, though I'm not sure it's the wrong word. What I was wrestling with internally certainly manifested itself externally.

DIANE: Had we not been married, had you found someone else

who felt exactly as you did, would your life have been easier or richer because of your lack of involvement in the world of theology, if you will?

JOHN: No, not richer. Certainly easier. Less problematic. This can be and is a difficult issue, so it would have been removed from what other issues the relationship or marriage might have had to deal with.

DIANE: But far less interesting.

JOHN: Well, that's right, far less interesting. And now, of course, looking back, since my conversion in 1979, now that I have a sense of the divine—

DIANE: —and now that you have a master's degree in theological studies—

JOHN: You and I now have some degree of common ground. I would define my Christianity in different ways from your Christianity. But nevertheless, we share, for example, Christmas and Easter services.

DIANE: Beyond that, we say grace at each meal. We give thanks to God for all of our blessings, for the health of our children and grandchildren, and you don't seem reluctant about that.

JOHN: Oh no. And I can say those things very genuinely. I'm overwhelmed by a daily sense of gratitude to some beneficent force.

DIANE: So what's changed?

JOHN: Well, me, that's what's changed. You and I can now hold hands and say grace in a way that I wouldn't have done at all, or about which I would have felt very awkward.

DIANE: It comes back to the question of religion and its interpretation. One can say that religion is the organized church. One can say that religion is the deep belief that one has in a spiritual being. It depends on how it's defined. The church is the most political institution out there, it turns me off, but that doesn't get in the way of my worshiping and receiving Holy Communion, and feeling the spirit of God in a church setting.

JOHN: And I have made the same distinction. One of the ironies is that now I'm the one who's more apt to want to go to church on Sundays than you. For a number of reasons, you now go less frequently than I. But when it comes to religion, I do think we've reached a meeting ground.

DIANE: Beyond that, you attend weekday services as well. So you're right, we've come a long way.

# Parenting

## John

I anticipated parenthood with three beliefs that I held deeply but barely discussed with Diane, if at all. First, children were an integral part of what would be our successful marriage. Second, loving one's children would be as easy as having them. Third, any ignorance about raising children would be overcome by patience and intelligence. These beliefs propelled me into parenthood, just nine months after we were married, with genuine joy and dangerous naïveté.

Diane and I experienced very different childhoods. However distant from each other, my mother and father doted on me. They supported and encouraged me, giving me wide latitude to do what I wanted. At times they imputed more maturity to me than I really had, but I had no doubt that they were in my corner, convinced that what I decided for myself would be good for me.

From what Diane told me, she was raised in a traditional Christian Arab household. Being a girl, it was ordained that her highest ambition was to be a wife and mother, in a role inferior to that of her husband. Any thought of attending college and pursuing a professional career was out of the question. In short, as I grew up my world was expanding, whereas Diane's was shrinking.

This disparity created serious problems for us as parents and, in turn, as spouses. Generally speaking, my tendency was to presume that our children were acting, or would act, responsibly. That act of faith corresponded to my childhood experience. Diane's inclination, on the other hand, was to doubt their ability to do the right thing. That, after all, was the way she had been treated as a girl.

This difference in presumptions had several consequences. It caused Diane to clash more with the children than I did. As a result, she tended to be cast as the "bad guy" and I as the "good guy." This made her resentful, especially as my absences placed a disproportionate burden on her. Perhaps in retaliation, Diane adopted the stratagem of imposing upon me the role of judge, with the responsibility of adjudicating between her and one or both of the children. I felt that this made me the "fall guy," whose decision was bound to disappoint one side or the other. Most of the time, I found myself siding with the children, which heightened the tension between Diane and me.

We also had different ideas about discipline. I was opposed to all forms of corporal punishment, including slapping or spanking. Throughout my childhood, I can recall only one occasion when my father cuffed me lightly on the back of my head. By contrast, Diane remembers being regularly hit not only with a hand or fist but with a metal spatula or wooden spoon. I was appalled when, in our son's early toddler days, Diane, following her parents' example, swatted David on his bottom. I insisted that there be no corporal punishment in our household. That quickly became the rule for the rest of our children's upbringing, a fact about which they both bragged to their young friends.

The children's privacy also emerged as an issue out of our respective pasts. As an only child, I had my own room, and it was tacitly understood that I could bar anyone from coming in—even my parents. Diane, by contrast, never had a room to herself until her sister married and moved away. Even then, she couldn't close her door, however much she wanted to. On one occasion, Jennie was furious with us and closed the door to her room, with a sign that read "Do Not Enter." Upon seeing the sign, Diane's immediate inclination was to assert parental authority, disregard the sign, and enter the room. I said that I felt it was terribly important for Jennie to have her own unconditional sense of privacy from all others, parents or otherwise. The door remained closed until Jennie chose to come out.

# Diane

One of the two most basic challenges most of us face as we attempt to move toward adulthood is parenting. The other: learning to live with another human being. It has been encouraging to watch today's young people share many of the responsibilities for parenting that, when John and I were married, fell to the wife alone. It was she who was expected to wash clothes, clean house, garden, prepare food, and, most importantly, take care of the child or children. I grew up with that model. It was the only one I knew, so I had no expectation that John would be involved in the day-to-day efforts of taking care of or raising our children. We've laughed and joked since then about the fact that, except for a period when I was in the hospital, before Jennie was born, John Rehm had never changed a diaper! How times have changed. Now I see our son-in-law, Russell, taking superb care of and responsibility for our grandson Benjamin. He doesn't hesitate to step forward to take over from Jennie when he senses he's needed. He doesn't have to be asked, he just does it.

The years of our children's infancy were a lonely time for me, since there were very few parents in our neighborhood who had young children. If there were questions to be asked or concerns to be shared, I was on the phone with the pediatrician. It seemed as though I started dialing the moment I knew his "telephone hour" began each morning, asking, I'm sure, some very basic questions, but at the same time trying to reassure myself that what I was doing as a parent, and how the child was behaving, were healthy and appropriate.

I've often wondered whether my extreme loneliness and sense of isolation would have been considerably reduced by the presence of close relatives and friends, people on whom I could call to ask the simplest questions or just to come for a visit. Both my mother and father were gone by then, John's mother was in New York, and I had left behind all my friends from my former marriage. I had grown up surrounded by aunts, uncles, and cousins, so the void I felt seemed particularly great. One neighbor across the street had young children, but she worked full time as a nurse, so we never managed to develop a relationship.

Since my own upbringing hadn't given me a sense of respect for myself as a child, in my ignorance I transferred those feelings and attitudes to the raising of my own children. I didn't assume they had rights of choice. I did assume that my choice, as the adult parent, was the operating principle. It was here that

John stepped in, with his own attitudes and upbringing as the backdrop. He argued that it was important to overlook the small transgressions. It was important to try to negotiate with each child, no matter what the issue happened to be. Food was an issue. Even as I recalled my own belligerent reaction to the foods my mother insisted I eat for breakfast, I foisted that same kind of rigid attitude on the children. Why should Jennie have to have scrambled eggs if she didn't like them? Weren't there acceptable substitutes? But somewhere deep inside me came the sense that children were expected to "obey," and it created many problems, both for me as a parent and for the two children.

By the time David reached adolescence, John was hardly to be found. He was either working or so angry with me that he left the house. He simply wasn't around. David and I had some extraordinarily difficult verbal battles, but most of the time he held his ground when he felt he was right. Then John would ultimately come in as the all-knowing arbiter and I would become furious, because most of the time he would take David's side. Those arguments left me shaken and weary, with a sense of defeat. I was the one against whom David rebelled in his adolescence, while his father seemed to be rebelling against me not only for David but for himself as well. It was a dreadful period.

Looking back, I must say that, considering the kinds of difficulties parents must deal with today, including drugs, alcohol, truancy, and violence, I believe that we were fortunate parents, both in terms of the times in which we lived and the integrity that our two children have. They went through tough times with me as a parent. At the same time, I've always felt that John should have played a stronger and more supportive role in the upbringing of our children.

# Dialogue on Parenting

JOHN: On this subject of parenting, I'd like to begin with an affirmative question, namely, what did we do right in raising Jennie and David? I'm so struck by how these two lovely, remarkable human beings have turned out. They have so many of the best kinds of qualities you can think of: honesty, integrity, compassion, the desire and the ability to help others. It's so easy to berate ourselves over all the wrong things we did that I thought it might be interesting to try to identify what we did right.

DIANE: Well, I think the two children had their own understanding of themselves, perhaps *in spite of* us—despite the difficulties we had with each other and despite the difficulties I had with them. Somehow, within each of them was a sense of what was right, how far they could go in testing us, how much they considered their own personal beings to be of value. I think that may be the essential thing we did right—to give each of them a sense of value.

JOHN: I would agree. I've often thought that while love is a vital and necessary part of what you give to children, it's not enough. You've got to give them a sense of self-worth, of their own dignity. This didn't come out of the air, but I don't know quite how we did it. I suppose if I had to say how, I would say that early on, with all the normal disciplinary problems, we gave them a sense that they were equal partners in our family of four, and had a significant and rightful position in that family.

DIANE: That was probably the part I had the most trouble with, given my own upbringing: feeling as though they were equal partners. I came into the marriage and into parenthood thinking there was this distance between parent and child. I began to understand that these were human beings who had their own internal life that was different from my idea of what it should be. Obviously there are basic approaches to life that parents try to instill in their children, but I finally came to realize that I could not impose my wishes or my instincts on them all the time.

JOHN: Speaking for myself, in terms of giving David and Jennie a sense of self-worth and spiritual equality, I may have gone too far in David's case, by imposing upon him obligations and responsibilities that were beyond his emotional age.

DIANE: Such as?

JOHN: The way we asked him at the age of nine or ten to baby-sit his younger sister.

DIANE: Well, yes, he was doing that, he was even cooking for his sister at that age. And of course, today, he adores cooking, working in the kitchen.

JOHN: He enjoys making lists. Jennie keeps her lists on her Palm Pilot. We taught both of them early on the importance of lists, to keep a household going.

DIANE: So maybe our need for a sense of order, our need for a sense of responsibility not only for oneself but for another, were communicated to them. In some ways, I think, Jennie, the younger child, "got away with" a lot more than David did, not only because she was the younger but because she was a girl. Somehow you expected more of David in terms of responsibility, and let more slack with Jennie.

JOHN: I did have a different relationship with Jennie and David.

You're right, I think, that she did have an easier time being a second child. But there was that period in her adolescence when, for some time, she was only an average student, with no particular desire to learn or excel.

DIANE: Whereas David excelled right from the start.

JOHN: And then, in her junior year of high school, she caught hold of herself and became a really serious student, to the point where not only was she able to get into a fine college, Carleton, but then went on to medical school. She stayed on that path. And we watched David go through graduate school to earn his doctorate in classical philosophy, and then use that learning to teach others to learn. Sooner or later, they both acquired this seriousness of purpose and a desire to help others. Above all, what so overwhelms me, almost to the point of tears, is that they reach out to others in both intellectual and emotional terms.

DIANE: We've been talking about the children and how they struggled through their own childhood and adolescence, and now have become these fine, strong adults. What we really haven't talked about is our relationship to ourselves and each other as parents. I think I had to struggle with my own feelings of deprivation as a child. For example, when David had the opportunity to go to Paris, I was furious because *I'd* never been to Paris! Here he was, just seventeen or so, and he was going off to Paris with his schoolmates. I couldn't believe it—and in retrospect, I cannot believe my own selfishness! You, as the good and generous father, felt very strongly that he should go, and so we argued. In the end, I could see the foolishness of the position I'd taken, and off he went for a glorious and enriching experience. So, in fact, you and I argued a lot about our approach to parenting. The basic question becomes: How do you work those things out beforehand? The answer is, you probably don't. You come upon parenting, each with a set of ideas and not even knowing you have those ideas. And there you are, facing parenthood, the most important responsibility in the world.

JOHN: Well, I suppose if I had to use one word to respond to your question, it would be communication. As two people move on from one point to another in the process of parenting, communication is indispensable if the process is going to make any sense.

DIANE: And you and I did not have that. All we seem to have done was to argue, almost every step of the way.

JOHN: Well, I think that communication did come into the process, although belatedly and with difficulty. In the early years, of course, I really wasn't there, and you were the effective parent. While I may have exerted some influence, it really wasn't a great deal. In later years, as they moved into adolescence, my recollection, Diane, is that you and I did discuss some of these issues. Don't you think there was some communication at work there?

DIANE: Yes, but I don't think you and I talked these things through to the extent that I hope parents are doing now. There are all kinds of books and lectures on parenting today, information regarding infancy, the "terrible twos," adolescence, right on up through early adulthood. You and I didn't take advantage of the literature available at the time, so we struggled with each other instead of turning to some external source of knowledge or wisdom.

JOHN: Do you think that really would have made a difference, if we had both sat down and read the same manual on parenting? I'm not sure it would have.

DIANE: But suppose we had gone to the same lecture on parenting, and an expert offered suggestions—it might have helped. But what you and I did was to knock heads.

JOHN: I come back to my basic point about communication. I agree that confrontation is not the best way to solve these issues. There should have been a more open communication, a reasoned sharing of problems and difficulties. But I think it's terribly important to hold on to the fact that, on balance, I think we did a pretty good job. The proof is in the pudding.

# Arguing

## John

Consider the following portrait of me as the husband and Diane as the wife. He was intellectually confident and emotionally immature. He placed great value upon words and their literal meaning. He believed that human intercourse demanded adherence to logic. As an only child who was rarely disciplined by his parents, he had little sense of the give-and-take of human relations. Without any significant experience of women prior to marriage, he had no reason to believe that he and his wife might observe different rules of argumentation. Indeed, when pressed, he would proclaim the superiority of rational discourse.

She was emotionally experienced and intellectually unsure. Before she was even twenty-two she had lost both her mother and father and obtained a divorce from her first husband. As a girl, she had been abused and had engaged in a constant yet suppressed battle with her parents. She was in touch with her feelings, light and dark, and equipped to express them forcefully. Although intellectually gifted and curious, she was intimidated by her husband's literacy and knowledge.

These conflicting traits and views were a recipe for recurrent misunderstandings in our marriage. The foundation for meaningful communication was fragile enough. Each of us was trying to establish a comfortable yet respected role in our relationship. Egos were easily bruised and all too often words became weapons rather than tools. Instead of shedding light, they gathered darkness. As our arguments became destructive, we both clung all the more strongly to our respective conceptions of useful dialogue. In fact, our "dialogues" frequently collapsed into destructive diatribes in which we both sought out new ways to use language to wound each other. My usual reaction at that point was simply to storm away from her, either withdrawing to my study or leaving the house.

It has taken me, unfortunately, a number of years to understand two fundamental aspects of constructive argumentation. First, listening is more important than speaking. I was typically intent on getting my own ideas across. In an effort to find common ground, I should have been listening to Diane; instead I was busy formulating in my mind the next salvo. This, in turn, would provoke Diane to respond in kind. Arguing broke down into a series of unilateral assertions, rather than bilateral exchanges.

Second, especially in the heat of argument, words are, at best, tentative clues to the speaker's thoughts. They are not to be viewed and used as precise indicators of a state of mind. Perhaps because of my legal training, I tended to turn any argument into an analysis of Diane's words. The more I did so, the more frustrated she became, since she felt that my approach complicated rather than clarified the problem. What I have finally begun to learn is that in such a setting, words are more exploratory than expository.

# Diane

Arguing has always been a part of my life. As a youngster, if I saw something unfair on the playing field I would shout out my displeasure. If there was a neighborhood friend with whom I was playing hopscotch, I would make sure to watch where she landed, and immediately challenge her if she landed on a line. I was even willing to risk her leaving the game altogether if she disagreed. In my high school sorority, it was I who argued passionately in favor of, or against, the acceptance of a new pledge. I was never reluctant to express my gut reactions—and let them fly—without pausing to assess how hurtful they might be, or how they might reflect on me.

At home, the story was a different one. There were no arguments between my parents, between my parents and me, or, in the open, between my sister and me. In truth, my sister and I fought constantly, but only when my parents weren't present, or when they were in another part of the house where they couldn't hear our squabbling. There were no opportunities to "argue" against my mother and father for a cause or a belief, or to protest what I perceived as an unfair decision. My parents ruled the kingdom, not only emotionally but physically, and that was that. Outside the house, I was able to express myself more openly, and I'm certain at times inappropriately.

During the early period of our courtship, there was no arguing between John and me. Instead, all of our finest qualities came to the surface, as I believe happens with many young couples. Rather than search out areas of difference, we discovered our similarities. When sparks of concern arose in my mind, I quickly buried them, fearing that I would somehow jeopardize the special relationship we seemed to have, and afraid of what might happen if John were to see my "real" self. If there were points of disagreement, they were addressed in a light and playful way. But later on in the courtship, and certainly before we were married, our different modes of argumentation came to the fore.

The aspects of John's personality that seemed to both attract and plague me most were his sense of independence and his belief that his primary allegiance was to his work. From the beginning of our dating period, I was struck by how free he seemed from the internal struggles regarding parental authority, which I continued to wage. It was profoundly revelatory to me that parents such as John's, who watched and supported rather than controlled, really existed. He hadn't gone through his life, as I had, feeling that his next move, whatever it was, could be disastrous. My feelings of independence came as a result of arguing, something I knew I could do and did well. I made others feel as if they had lost, while I felt triumphant.

That might work in some areas, but it certainly didn't work in our marriage. Because I found myself frustrated and lonely in the early years of our marriage, I believed the only way I could make a "connection" with John was through argument, and argue I did, when I could—when he was around—which, in turn, made him not want to be around very much at all.

# Dialogue on Arguing

JOHN: Diane, after more than forty years of marriage, I'm still learning how to argue, by which I mean to argue in a constructive sense. I've yet to fully learn that one should listen more than talk, stick to the issue, and not, as I like to put it, universalize the issue into "You *never* do this," or "You *always* do that." To keep one's cool, to be open to legitimate compromise, which respects the views of both parties. Married people, or those in long-term relationships, do argue about both lesser or greater issues. I wish I'd taken Argumentation 101.

DIANE: [*laughter*] Well, I'm afraid I did go to Argumentation 101 way back when I was a kid. Certainly, arguing with my sister, something you didn't do, or *not* being able to argue with my parents but finding ways to resist them. So then you came along with your admonition of "Stick to the words! Stick to the definition! Stick to the narrow focus of the argument." All that used to drive me crazy, because arguments are about more than just the issue at hand. Whether it's moving a spoon from one setting to another, whether it's putting clothes in one place or another, there's always some underlying issue. And you were belittling my feelings about the issue. You wanted to stick to the facts, and the facts weren't the only things of interest to me.

JOHN: What you've just said stimulates two thoughts. First, I didn't have any grounding in arguing, because I was an only child. I didn't have to battle with siblings. And second, when it came to me and my desires and my interests, there was no arguing on the part of my parents. They were very indulgent. They were happy and content to let me be who I was. So I didn't grow up in an atmosphere of argumentation, as I think you did.

DIANE: What about your playmates? Other young boys?

JOHN: I ran around with a gang of boys, but no, I don't recall much arguing there. At school, we exchanged ideas and engaged in intellectual argumentation, to be sure. But what you and I are talking about is arguing that, to a greater or lesser degree, is based on some foundation of feelings. That's another thing I've had to learn, which I think you've taught me. It's that the words are only a hint of what the individual is getting at, that there are underlying feelings, and that part of successful arguing is to be willing to pursue and expose such feelings.

DIANE: And what I had to learn was not to attack you, not to take the issue at hand and turn it into a "Oh, you never . . ." or "You always . . ." Not to attack you as a human being, but to try to stay within the framework of the issue. I think therapy helped a great deal. The other factor that helped was that in therapy you learned that if I presented an issue to you, you didn't have to solve it immediately. You could simply listen to me. It used to bother the hell out of me that I would try to offer up some problem of mine and you'd be off dissecting it. What you were doing was not listening to the feelings behind what I was offering. You were moving on to problem solving.

JOHN: I believe women may be closer to their feelings and able to recognize that while the issue may seem essentially rational, there is this underlay of feelings to be pursued. That was a novel idea for me. I thought that argument was an aspect of rational discourse. In a sense, it was supposed to depart from, or even override, the feelings because it was in the rational domain.

DIANE: Which is how you got to your famous line, "What would Aristotle think?" In the middle of an argument, I was going on and on about something, and you stood there laughing at me, and uttered that question. Which just threw me into a huge fit.

JOHN: That was a neat way of encapsulating my approach to argumentation, which was to stress the rational or pseudo-rational, because that was my strength. Emotionally, I was not mature and had difficulty dealing with the more emotional aspects of whatever we were arguing about.

DIANE: I was really the first person, then, in your life who questioned your way of arguing and, in particular, your focus on the words instead of the feelings.

JOHN: I thought that the words and their dictionary meanings would provide the ground for argumentation. But what that leaves out, of course, is what we've been talking about: these underlying feelings have to be acknowledged if an issue is going to be fully explored and solved through dissension. So I retreated to what I believed was rational discourse, and that didn't serve your needs at all. In fact, it tended to cut off the expression of your more emotional side.

DIANE: I guess the basic question becomes: Why do you think you and I argued as much as we did?

JOHN: I think most couples do argue a lot. We just don't see it, or they don't care to admit it. But I've thought about the same question. I think you and I became competitive quite quickly in our relationship and in our arguments. It was a kind of childish need to prevail, to be right, to be the one who wins. In your essay, you bring out that strain in you. As I've already said, I was brought up to believe, "Well, *of course* Scoop is right!"

DIANE: [*laughter*] You used to say to me during our courtship how much fun it was having a "little sister." All of a sudden, what you had lacked—the adolescent rivalry and tug-of-war that normally go on in a family between siblings—began to happen between you and me. And, of course, I'd had a lot of experience as a younger sister. So I was ready to fight back.

JOHN: In terms of my own parents, I really didn't see them engaged in argumentation, the give-and-take that is the heart of honest argumentation. Each had a separate and independent domain and tended to stay there. Not only was I brought up to believe I was always right, but my parents' model was one of nonarguing. My approach was bound to run right into yours.

DIANE: It ran right into me, someone who had not been able to talk back to my parents but argued secretly with my sister. You and I never had any physical encounters, but the loudness of the arguments did become childish—I'm going to get you, and you're going to get me. We wasted so much time arguing.

JOHN: I think the arguing arose from a certain defensiveness on my part, particularly when it was a matter of coming up against you, because you are a strong person. I really wasn't well equipped to engage in marital argument, and it's taken us a long time to reach the point where we can listen rather than talk, stick to the issue, and render argument constructive.

DIANE: And when we can't render it constructive, perhaps just to keep quiet and walk away from it, cool off, and come back to it later, maybe with a little humor, which I find myself doing these days.

# Friends

## John

Family and friends. In our daily conversation, the two words seem naturally complementary. Their very alliteration enhances the sense of closeness. A family without friends is marooned. Friends without family are adrift. Our society therefore expects the two to draw together over time into an extended family.

I believe that Diane, consciously or otherwise, has embraced this model. On the one hand, she possesses a fierce sense of loyalty to our immediate family. Its internal struggles do not, in her view, threaten loyalty; instead they call for greater efforts to maintain the family's unity. On the other hand, Diane is deeply committed to her friends—both male and female. She has played the major role in building our extended family. As a result, she has many genuine friends in a city that discourages lasting relationships. Diane's affection for others occupies a continuum that blurs such distinctions as close friend and good friend.

My conception of friends is less generous and therefore more restrictive. I tend to create a hierarchy of closeness. That hierarchy highlights the superiority of family over friends. Moreover, it establishes degrees of closeness among friends. Indeed, in a given group of people we know, Diane would count more friends and I would have more acquaintances. When greeting strangers, Diane sees the opportunities for lowering the bars to friendship. I, on the other hand, am inclined to keep the bars up and see what, if anything, happens.

These differences in our approach to family and friends have often created rifts between us. In a typical case, we receive an invitation from a couple we know. Diane considers them friends—or at least potential friends—and wants to accept. I regard them as acquaintances at best, and am lukewarm about extending our already large "family of friends." In this situation, the consequences are all too predictable. If I go, I'll be unhappy. If I don't go, Diane will be unhappy. In either case, the unhappiness is apt to spill over and distort our own relationship.

Yet, as we have discovered, compromises are possible. If the occasion is more of a business affair, Diane may go alone. If we can agree to limit the time of attendance, I am more likely to go. If we learn that good friends will also be present, we're both more comfortable. In short, the invitation does not need to trigger another skirmish between Diane, the party girl, and John, the recluse.

# Diane

If I didn't have my friends, I would feel bereft. In some cases, I have felt my friends, both male and female, to be closer to me than members of my own family. Friends have always been a part of my life, from childhood playmates to adolescent sorority sisters to companions in the workplace, and now to friends of up to thirty, forty, and even fifty years. They are part of who I am and who I have become. I have absorbed parts of them in my actions, in my behaviors, in my attitudes.

Earlier in this book, in writing about arguing and the differences between John and me, I spoke of my willingness to get in there and fight the battle. Partly through my friends, I've learned how better to hear the "other," and to present my arguments in ways that can be heard, rather than in ways that seek to defeat the other. I've come to understand the generosity that comes from extending the hand of friendship. Those whom I have loved as friends, and those who have loved me, have taught me kindness, have helped me soften my approach, have informed my vision, both of myself and the hurdles I've faced. Without those friendships, I would be a very different person, both personally and professionally, from who I am today.

Each morning at around seven, the phone rings. It is my dear friend Jane Dixon, currently the Bishop pro tempore of the Diocese of Washington. For more than thirty years now, these daily phone calls have helped me to face each day. Our conversations are necessarily brief since both of us are heading into a new day at the office, but they are extraordinarily helpful and even uplifting. Whether there is a specific problem or a general unease, it can be expressed and even worked on, however briefly. What comes through in those five minutes or so is the love and support we feel for one another, the caring and the nurturing that we can offer to carry us through another challenging day. When we're on our separate vacations, we try to check in occasionally, just to catch up.

There are other friends, equally important to me, and, I

daresay, to John, though I'm not sure he really recognizes that. The friendships tend to come through me because he is apt to be less sociable, and less willing to open his life to the demands of new interactions that are more than superficial. Occasionally he will meet up with someone he finds interesting, but he won't pursue that acquaintanceship to create a true friendship.

At this point in my life, I do wonder how much more broadly my friendships can extend. I realize how much time and energy it takes to maintain a friendship. It takes real work to be more than an acquaintance. Up to now, I've been willing to make that effort, but I also know my plate is full.

# Dialogue on Friends

JOHN: Marriage changes its participants in a number of ways, some obvious, some not so obvious. In terms of our marriage, Diane, I'm struck by the fact that my life would have been really different if I hadn't had you to introduce me to people, to reach out to people, and to form friendships with people. At the end of my essay on friendship, I talk about you as the party girl and me as the recluse. That may be an exaggeration, but not too much so. Without marrying you, I think I would have led a lone—maybe lonely—life.

DIANE: Without me there wouldn't have been real friends in your life?

JOHN: Oh, probably a few, I would guess. But the countervailing strain in me is strong, based upon my childhood experiences.

DIANE: So, beyond your professional relationships—for example, I think of your partner, David Busby, whom you love like a brother—would you have found ways to open your life to allow others in?

JOHN: David is a good case study. Assuming you and I weren't married and I had David as a partner in our law firm, yes, I would have gotten to know him more, with some degree of closeness. But not with the degree of intimacy we've had, largely because of you, and the creation of a close relationship among the four of us, you and I, David and Mary Beth.

DIANE: And, of course, Mary Beth feels much as I do, and frankly, so does David as well. They're both gregarious persons, and the two of them welcomed us into their social circle, as well as into their family, from the earliest moments we met them more than thirty years ago. But I want to go beyond that, because I wonder about ordinary friendships among males, and whether friendship is a different concept for you as a man than it is for me as a woman. I can think of some men who enjoy real friendships with other men. You, on the other hand, with few exceptions, haven't really extended yourself into a male world.

JOHN: I think I'm the exception, not the rule. Men, by and large, do establish friendships of varying degrees and do things with other men—sports activities like golf and tennis. In my case, I tend to shun others, believing I'm probably more interesting than people I meet. That may be false, but that's my feeling.

DIANE: It's also arrogant!

JOHN: Yes, there's some arrogance, I would agree. But that's the way I am. In some ways, my best friends are you, David, and Jennie. One test of a real friendship is, To whom would you turn instinctively, without thought, if you had a serious problem on your hands? I would turn immediately to my family, much less so to friends outside the family. I don't think that's true of you. I think there are a number of friends to whom you would turn, as well as to members of your family.

DIANE: Of course, because they are as close to me as members of my family. I have both female and male friends to whom I know I could turn in case of emergency. But it's not just that. Each of these people has helped me see the world in a different way. Each has opened a window toward attitudes and thinking about the world and other people. Sometimes I fear you are closed to friendships because you are *fearful*.

JOHN: No, I don't think fearful is the right word. Rather, it's a sense that the effort will not be productive, that it will all too often fall back on small talk, which you know I dislike and see as a waste of time. Much of the kind of conversation you have with your close friends I wouldn't have because it wouldn't interest me. You're taken up—and I say this with some admiration—with the richness of diurnal events. I'm not there. I just read a book review on the history of the British Empire. I found my five minutes reading that book review really rewarding. I don't have that kind of experience with many people. Now, you may say, "You haven't tried hard enough," and maybe that's true. But at some point early in my life, I decided that, on my own, I could be an interesting fellow.

DIANE: To yourself. But what that does is to create a narrow worldview. You actually have one of the broadest understandings of this world of anyone I know, yet at the same time, your views come through the printed word, listening to music, and the like, and not so much through exchanges with other people. Then, all of a sudden, you'll have an exchange with someone who's totally outside the bounds of friendship and be really intrigued.

JOHN: But you see, my exchanges are with the people who compose music, write literature, create art—those are the people with whom I communicate best, although I am interacting with their works and not the persons themselves.

DIANE: But that's not quite true. You told me recently, talking about your work as a volunteer at the Hospice of Washington, about a woman who was dying. You came home and said to me, "She's a very interesting woman." Now what's the difference here? That's why I use the word "fearful." It's as though you're fearful of becoming involved as a friend with another person. Yet you're willing to have personal exchanges that don't draw you in for the long term.

JOHN: That's well put. If it's a fear, it's a fear of beginning what seems to be a potentially interesting relationship and then having it founder because the person doesn't show that much interest or lacks the kind of enthusiasm for music and art that I would want to see. Maybe I've been disappointed in the past—maybe that's one of the reasons why I'm inhibited. You know, this is a fascinating topic for me, because, as is so often the case, you and I come at these topics from such different points of view. That's particularly true in the case of friendship. On the other hand, I value the friendships that I've been able to cultivate because of you.

DIANE: And here's what fascinates me: you say you value the friendships you've been able to cultivate because of me, yet you go on downplaying the value of friendship, and remain more or less aloof from it. You say you don't like small talk and find it boring. Yet in that "small talk" can lie some of the largest ideas a person can offer. Sometimes I find myself digging for nuggets, looking for keys to what this person is really all about. It becomes a fascinating game, with some true surprises awaiting me. If I could express one wish here, it would be that in the future you would make a greater effort to engage more fully in friendship, and to relax your somewhat remote posture. I know that, deep down, the idea of the "loner" appeals to you, because of the parental models you've talked about. But at some point, to be really free to become our own adult selves, don't we have to shed those parental models and become our own persons? We still have time to change and, perhaps, become better friends, to each other as well as to others.

# Vacations

## John

Among marital pitfalls, vacations can prove to be a big one. The word "vacation" derives from the Latin word for "freedom." In keeping with this etymology, we anticipate a respite from everyday cares. However contradictory our past experience may be, we're confident that the next vacation will be a success. We take comfort in the fragile smiles on last year's photographs. We're armed with a fresh resolve to have fun. So why does the reality so often fall short of the anticipation?

In my experience, this shortfall is largely the product of anxieties that the two of us bring to vacations. We have difficulty dealing with these anxieties, since they are deep-seated and therefore not readily perceived. Moreover, even when they reveal themselves, we're likely to avoid discussing them because of the sensitivities associated with them. To inject them into our vacation plans seems unnecessarily gloomy.

Vacations make me particularly anxious about the management of time. Ironically, they're supposed to reduce our preoccupation with the passing of hours and days, yet I'm intent on filling each day with historical and cultural experiences. This calls for the allocation of available time, the preparation of a schedule, and the curtailment of diversions. I see this procedure as a rational way of enriching our vacation. Diane, on the other hand, rebels against it as a form of regimentation that spoils the anticipated pleasure. At times we've successfully negotiated our way through our differences. At other times, they've proven obdurate, and we have each struck out on our own.

Vacations can impose what feels to me like enforced intimacy. I'm expected to spend morning, noon, and night with my wife, a demand that's not part of our day-to-day relations. I'm reminded of the old chestnut, "I married you for better or for worse, but not for lunch." The adjustment is all the more trying because it's so abrupt. Within a few hours of leaving home, I'm expected to thrive on this unaccustomed familiarity. Without goodwill and injections of humor, the new regime can make me feel confined and even trapped. Moreover, there are few opportunities that will permit me to escape in a way that will not make Diane feel rejected.

Vacations also require that I cope with Diane's fears about our personal well-being. During trips, and particularly those abroad, Diane has diverse fears of varying degrees of intensity. She is afraid, for example, that we will miss our plane or bus or train, have our luggage stolen, get lost in a strange city, be cheated by the taxi driver, pay too much for a gift, use the wrong exchange rate, or be mugged in a crowd. On some occasions, I believe these fears are legitimate. They may properly call for special precautions, and I don't resent her insistence on them.

On other occasions, however, her fears strike me as unwarranted and downright silly. As she harps on them, I get annoyed and even angry. I try to rationally explain why she needn't be anxious, and I receive an irritated reply. The day risks being spoiled unless we can remember to talk with—and not at—each other about our anxieties.

# Diane

In the past few years, John and I have experienced a variety of vacations: trips abroad, trips around this country, traveling alone, with friends, or to our farm. Perhaps the anticipation of trips abroad has, for the most part, been more joyful than the experiences themselves—with one exception. In 1984, to celebrate our twenty-fifth wedding anniversary, John and I traveled to Italy for the first time, to Florence and Venice, and then to Paris, where our son, David, was working to help John's law firm establish its Paris office. In my memory, that trip was absolutely perfect, with its ease of travel, reliability of connections, and breathtaking experiences of those glorious cities. I was stunned by the beauty of Florence and Venice, yet taken aback by their differences. It took me a day or so to adjust to Venice, but once I had, I felt myself becoming a part of the Grand Canal, the gondolas, the flowers, every sight, sound, and smell of that city. I fell in love all over again with my husband, and with everything around me.

John travels far more easily than I. By that I mean he is basically assertive, and without trepidation. I, on the other hand, am generally fearful, whether we're traveling by car, train, boat, or plane. Basically, the fear is of losing my way. When we're abroad, for example, I find myself reaching for John's hand far more often than I would in a familiar city. I don't read maps well, so I have no sense of where we are or where we should be headed. Perhaps I rely too much on him. I feel myself becoming more of a child when we travel together, assuming that he'll make sure that everything that should happen will happen. For the most part, I can say that we have never had any truly unpleasant experiences while traveling, except for one trip to the farm.

The children were small, perhaps David was seven and Jennie four. We were driving up to the farm in our roomy yellow Plymouth, with our long-haired dachshund plus two cats in the backseat with the children. This was before the age of mandatory seat belts, mind you, so the crate with the cats sat between the children, and the dog was either in back or in the front seat with me. In addition, there was a car-top carrier loaded with equipment we needed each time we went to the farm. It was raining, not terribly hard, but the roads were slick. The speed limit was fifty-five miles per hour, but even that seemed too fast to be traveling in those weather conditions. John was driving, and I asked him to slow down a bit. He did somewhat, but just at that point the car hit a particularly wet area and we literally began to plane. We took off! I could feel the car lose traction, leave the ground, and then, suddenly, spin three hundred and sixty degrees in the air! Fortunately, we landed in a slight ditch on the right shoulder, facing in the right direction. The good Lord was surely with us that day. Immediately upon landing, all of us were stunned and shocked, and John said, "Is everybody all right?" And then, in the stillness of that frightful moment, the children began to giggle. Not only were they "all right," they saw the incident, now that they were safe, as something like a thrill ride at an amusement park. The cats were meowing, the dog was barking, and we were all safe! The car-top carrier had swerved off the top of the car, and much of its contents had landed on the right shoulder along with us. Passing cars stopped to offer help, but we managed to retrieve everything and stuff it into the car—all but the car-top carrier itself, which had to be abandoned.

I shall never forget that experience, because it taught me that in a single instant, life can be forever changed. I suppose I've always had that fear, and that day it was confirmed.

Another difficult aspect of travel for me is leaving home. I love the comfort and the beauty of our home and our garden. I love the freedom of movement, and the familiarity of our environment. I know where I can travel and move relatively safely. I can shop, I can go to movies and restaurants, I can be with the people I know and love.

When we go away together, I'm apt to be *only* with John, and while that can hold promise, there are many times I'd rather not be with him. He can be moody and very quiet, especially when we're at the farm. I love the peace and quiet of the farm, but there are times when I want more companionship through conversation. There are certainly times when he's willing to converse, but at other moments, his responses to my questions or comments can be very brief and not particularly welcoming. When I perceive his mood to be withdrawn, I've learned to ignore him and turn to other activities. I've gotten better at that through the years. Especially when we're alone, as at the farm, it has become a learning process for me to fall back on my own resources and cease to depend on him for my entertainment.

# Dialogue on Vacations

DIANE: I want to start by saying that this vacation, here for three weeks at the farm and working together on this book, may be the best vacation I can recall. Being together yet going our separate ways as we've worked, being quiet when we've chosen to be, it's just been delightful. Unfortunately, that's not the way vacations have always been in the past. First of all, we've both had the difficulty of making the transition from work to play. You and I don't play together easily. It's not easy for either of us to *totally* relax, and I think that's part of the problem.

JOHN: I think it was during a vacation at Caneel Bay in the Virgin Islands that we learned our lesson. There was really nothing to do but swim, sail, eat, and drink in an admittedly lovely setting. But the lack of intellectual stimulation and activity left us snarling at each other. In one of my solitary walks, I came upon the remains of a dead goat. This somehow typified the vacation.

DIANE: Yes, it became clear that we need a mixture of relaxation and cultural stimulation to create an enjoyable vacation—with the exception of the farm, where there is a combination of various activities, such as physical work, long walks, reading, and food preparation.

JOHN: One of our major difficulties has been what I call the enforced intimacy of a vacation. Being at the farm is a good example of that, because it's just the two of us, trying to arrange our days in a pleasurable way. I do agree we've managed to do that particularly well on this occasion, because we're both genuinely and deeply dedicated to the project of writing the book. But as you say, each of us has found time to do separate things. We've been together, and we've been apart. Trips abroad, on the other hand, have demanded that we be with each other all the time. I think, in that respect, we've grown and learned. You're now more willing to have me go off for two hours or so to see a special exhibition, while you may be with a friend and do some window-shopping. So that degree of accommodation has been accomplished.

DIANE: I wonder whether we're all that different from other couples, or whether we just expected too much. Perhaps I expected too much. Perhaps I fantasized each time that a vacation would be "perfect." Vacations are never perfect. Take, for example, the early years, when we used to take the kids to the beach each summer. That was marvelous. But on the other hand, you didn't like going out in the sun because of your skin, so you would go down to the beach early in the morning and late in the afternoon, whereas I wanted to sit down on the beach all day.

JOHN: True. And that annoyed you at times. But you've touched on the illusion of the perfect vacation. I think we all suffer from that. You mention other couples. Looking back, I can think of good friends of ours, couples who have sound relationships, who would show irritation and annoyance over petty matters while vacationing. I think it's difficult for people to spend time in this enforced intimacy. They're going to get on each other's nerves to a degree. But at the same time, I wouldn't take the illusion away from the vacation, because that's part of the fun. The trick is to understand and recognize that the illusion will be impaired to some degree. You roll with the punch and let the vacation continue.

Diane: Sometimes it's hard to roll with the punch. In the last few years, you and I have taken shipboard vacations with other couples. The first time we looked at the size of the cabin we were going to be in, I almost fainted! It was no more than six feet across, with hardly any room between the beds. We could barely pass each other in the room. And then the bathroom!

John and Diane: [laughter]

Diane: It had a kind of combination shower, toilet, everything. It was enforced intimacy to a degree even I found almost intolerable.

John: And yet, Diane—this was our Russia trip, from Moscow to St. Petersburg, all by water, through canals, lakes, and rivers—I look back on that as one of our most successful vacations. We were able to transcend the incredible exiguity—

Diane: [laughter]

John: —of our "stateroom." Of course, being with friends does help. It can ease the situation and relieve the enforced intimacy to some degree. I can remember that each friend of ours on that trip wrestled with the same problem.

Diane: Thinking about friends in another context and looking back on our trips to the beach, I used to love to invite *everybody* down there. At one point we must have had twenty people in that apartment. There must have been ten or twelve kids sleeping on the floor in sleeping bags. I loved every minute of it. It was fun looking around seeing everybody, but I think you had some problems with it.

JOHN: No question, it was difficult. That situation certainly encroached upon my need for more privacy, more time to be alone, to walk on the beach. But at the same time—and this is part of what you've brought to our marriage, which I really do appreciate—even then, I had fun. For example, I can recall the two of us making breakfast—

DIANE: —for everyone!

JOHN: You were the short-order chef, and we were very fussy. We had a menu for each individual, whether it was scrambled or fried eggs, bacon, toast, muffins—all of it. That was quite a piece of theater, which I enjoyed at the time.

DIANE: So now perhaps you might want to take a vacation that I'd rather not take. I'm not sure I want to visit some of the far-off, more exotic countries I know you'd like to see. I have reservations about food and health. I'm worried about traveling to certain areas of the world. I think I'd like to see more of this country.

JOHN: That's a new thought, that I might go off on a vacation alone, and I must say, my initial reaction is quite negative. For all the difficulties you and I have had on such trips—and we've had difficulties—I've enjoyed the companionship with you and sharing the exploration, the new events. I would be sad not to have you there to share in that experience.

DIANE: But I do think we're going to have to negotiate vacations. This notion of "We're going here" or "We're going there" has to be one of agreement for the vacation to have any chance of satisfying both people.

JOHN: You've used for me what is the key word, "negotiate." In that sense, a vacation is a test of a marital relationship—not a huge test, but a significant one.

DIANE: Do you think it always was in our case?

JOHN: A test? Oh yes, and over the years I think we've learned that negotiation is the key, not that we've always succeeded in achieving an effective negotiation. But a vacation does require a series of compromises, adjustments, accommodations—indeed, negotiations—if both parties are going to derive some pleasure from it.

DIANE: I would remind you of a trip we took together to Montreal. You and I were so angry with each other. We went into a restaurant together for a cup of tea, and you said, "I want to go home, and you can stay here." I said, "I'm not staying here by myself." And then somehow, after we hammered that out—and I remember a waiter hovering nervously nearby, not knowing whether to ask us for our order or not—somehow we came back to our hotel room and had the most glorious meal from room service. I didn't feel like going out to dinner—

JOHN: —and you had on your nightgown—

DIANE: —and we just sat there in our room and had that wonderful meal. It was really incredible.

JOHN: It was incredible. We covered the full spectrum, from this intense dislike—we didn't even want to look at each other—to this wonderful dinner, and fun conversation. I may have had broiled salmon. . . .

DIANE: I had rack of lamb.

JOHN: That's a warm and enduring memory. For me, vacations

are a microcosm of a marriage. So many people don't recognize that, or they push it aside. But if people could view vacations that way, I think they would tend to have a better time. The illusion wouldn't be so great, but the reality would be more rewarding.

# Criticism

## John

What are some of the modes of behavior that can corrode a marriage? Several come immediately to my mind—indifference, silence, and anger. All three are variants of psychological abuse. That is, they are willfully inflicted, they are designed to cause pain, and—worst of all—they give the inflicting party at least momentary pleasure. If the relationship contains a degree of vitality, that pleasure will turn into nausea.

In the past, though less so today, Diane and I have used criticism of each other as a corrosive agent. I'm not talking about criticism that is offered and received in a constructive way. If we are feeling relatively secure in our relationship, Diane's criticism of me need not be divisive, and can, in fact, bolster our relationship. At the very least, it can provide a basis for exploring whether the criticism is valid and, if so, what steps can be taken to address its cause.

The criticism I have in mind is destructive and typically reveals three stages. First, it has an objective pretext. For example, I may criticize Diane for accepting one too many invitations. Or Diane may criticize me for not having replaced frayed shirts with new ones. In each case, the criticism has some initial validity.

Second, the criticism provokes an exchange that broadens the complaint at hand. Almost before we know it, I'm accusing Diane of not taking into account my limited tolerance for socializing, and Diane is taking me to task for not being sufficiently sensitive to her desire that I look presentable. Initially the criticism was fueled by irritation and directed to a particular issue. Now the criticism taps into animosity and attacks an aspect of the other's personality. Objectivity has become subjective, and the specific has turned into the general. Voices are raised, and comments become increasingly personal.

Third, the now heated debate resorts to what I call the vocabulary of the absolute. I find myself characterizing Diane as being "always" self-centered and authoritarian. For her part, she depicts me as "never" caring about her feelings and attempting to hurt her through my lack of sartorial attention. For a few minutes, my sweeping condemnation of Diane gives me a perverse sense of power and pleasure. As emotions cool, I am saddened—even sickened—by my words. I wonder how I could have so exaggerated such a minor, seemingly soluble problem.

The fact is, I'm particularly sensitive to Diane's criticism. More than anyone else, she can get under my skin and make me feel less than competent. For the most part, her criticisms tend to be minor, and I have learned not to react immediately to their sting. A pause gives both of us the opportunity to prevent the issue from getting out of hand. By keeping it in its original context, we stand a chance of addressing it in a constructive way.

# Diane

I grew up hearing constant criticism, from my parents and from my family generally. My hair was too curly, too filled with tangles, and unkempt. My dresses were wrinkled. My face was dirty. My voice was too loud. My friends made too much noise in the house. My fingers were ridiculously long. I was a tomboy. Every aspect of my life came under parental scrutiny and criticism. Teachers, on the other hand, gave me praise and support. Nevertheless, it was my parents' behavior that established the pattern I carried into my marriage to John.

John grew up assuming that everything he did was exemplary in the eyes of his parents. When I came along and began to criticize, for example, his lack of attention to his frayed collars, his worn-out shoes, his heavy glasses, I guess it was the first time in his life he'd heard any such criticism. I held back nothing, and didn't hesitate to deliver those criticisms in a stern, sometimes mocking voice. He was always immaculately groomed, but what he wore was of little interest to him.

Likewise, if there was a moment in a restaurant when I perceived that his voice was getting too loud, I would try to shush him. It reached a point where he would actually get louder, just to spite me. Or, in a much less public setting, if I felt he was careless with the dishes as he emptied the dishwasher, I would say so, and probably not in a very kind way. That would lead to an argument, a bitter exchange of words, and, ultimately, slammed doors and silence.

As my criticisms of John intensified in the early years of our marriage, he fought back, with comments about how I looked, my complexion, how I kept house, anything at all he knew would hurt me. I knew the children were affected, because after one of these bitter back-and-forth exchanges, they would come to the dinner table very quietly, feeling that what had been said had somehow undercut their sense of security in the household. It was a horrible way to live, and we had to find a way to stop it.

## Dialogue on Criticism

JOHN: This issue is a really rough one for me, for several reasons. I grew up without experiencing criticism. To almost a literal degree, in my parents' eyes and in my own, I could do no wrong. There was no need to criticize me. And based on my recollection, my father and mother didn't handle criticism from the other very well. It either sparked emotional conflict of one kind or another or else moody silences, so I didn't have a good model for dealing with criticism and therefore was badly unprepared as I entered into marriage with you.

DIANE: I think when you're in the throes of love, your emotions take over. When the day-to-day living process comes down to reality, the criticism comes all too easily and all too often. I do agree that you were hypersensitive to most any criticism. My failure was not to realize early on just how sensitive you were, because of your background and upbringing. I had no idea that I was the first person in the world who had ever criticized you. I had come from a household where everything I did was criticized. It came too easily for me, sadly, until we reached a point where we couldn't even speak to each other anymore. We reached a terrible impasse because of criticism.

JOHN: Because of my lack of experience and preparation, even the smallest issue that you might raise almost immediately went beyond the bounds of the issue itself. In most cases, the issue was probably valid. But in my case, there was an immediate leap from the issue itself to a presumed *attack* on my integrity, value, and worth. In emotional terms, small issues had a way of exploding and suddenly raising the authenticity of my own self.

DIANE: Can you think of an example?

JOHN: Yes, as you'll recall, we periodically met with David's teachers. They didn't see any need to do so, because David was such a fine student. But we wanted to keep up with his progress through their eyes. On one occasion, we were scheduled to meet at a given time. Because of events at the office that I couldn't control, I got home late, thus making the teachers wait for us beyond the appointed time. As we got into the car, you began immediately to berate me. I think I may have tried briefly to explain my predicament at the office, but in the face of your continued carping, I exploded and repeatedly yelled, "F—— you." The windows of the car were wide open, so that anyone who happened to be near could certainly hear my words and my rage. I eventually subsided, but it was a good example of an intensity of anger that went well beyond the issue at hand—the time of our meeting—and tapped into underlying problems of much greater severity.

DIANE: I remember that so vividly. Without therapy, I think we might have separated over the issue of criticism, because it became such a central part of the difficulties between us. You inferred criticism from even the slightest hint of a question. Even now, I have to say to you, "Scoop, I'm just asking you a question. I'm not criticizing you." So after forty-two years of marriage, I realize that you still have that sensitivity. I don't know if it's a matter of how each of us grew up, but what we finally had to come to was a written contract.

JOHN: A written contract that essentially said, "I will not criticize you . . ." in the slightest way or over the smallest issue for a given period of time.

DIANE: And we kept having to revise and update the contract, over a period of time. We'll include the first version of the contract following our dialogue.

JOHN: Certainly for me that was a breakthrough, to be in an environment where I was neither the one who criticized nor the one being criticized. It was a kind of truce, and it had some healing qualities.

DIANE: It was difficult to get you to sign it at first. We were in New Hampshire, and I said to you, "Are you ready to sign this contract?" And you screamed back at me, "I don't know." So it was not an easy process, as though we just had to draw up a contract and everything would be fine after that. There was a *war* going on within this marriage, and criticism was a central weapon of the war.

JOHN: And why did there have to be the war at all?

DIANE: Because we came from such different backgrounds, with such different perspectives about what a relationship was. I think you came to the relationship thinking you would continue with the independence of thought, you would continue with your sense of self-acceptance, and acceptance by others—namely, me—of your behavior, attitude, voice, dress, everything. And when I raised any objections whatsoever, you became furious.

JOHN: Do you think you were excessive in your criticism of me?

DIANE: I think I became so. There was escalation going on.

JOHN: Why did you have to take the route of escalation?

DIANE: Because I couldn't reach you.

JOHN: So out of frustration and the like—

DIANE: And nonresponsiveness—

JOHN: Well, that's true. Nonresponsiveness to criticism certainly existed in my family, and I suppose I drew on that experience.

DIANE: You drew on that experience, and used nonresponsiveness as a way to shield yourself from my criticism.

JOHN: And, of course, nonresponsiveness was also consistent with my normal inclination to withdraw when difficulties arose. But looking back, with all the benefit of hindsight, what should we have done to avoid the extreme frustration and severe escalation that developed?

DIANE: It would be interesting to outline a series of questions for young people or older people considering a long-term relationship to integrate into their own conversations before they enter that relationship. What if I had asked you, before we were married, "What role did criticism play in your life as you were growing up?" and you had said to me, "Absolutely none. No one ever criticized me for anything."

JOHN: That would have raised a flag, and we could have pursued that issue.

DIANE: Exactly. And in my case, totally the opposite of yours, criticism became part of a way of life.

JOHN: This is consistent with my theory that people are fearful and in some ways almost childlike deep down. If you lack self-confidence, or your confidence is less than adequate, then I think criticism can all too readily be taken—not necessarily correctly, but nevertheless taken—as an assault upon the self. So maybe you're right, Diane. If we could have begun to discuss that issue, which I think is so loaded, that might have eased things for us later on.

DIANE: I can recall going together to various events when you and I weren't even speaking, because of some element of criticism. Those long periods of not even talking came about largely as a result of criticism, some form of rejection of the other because of criticism. I wonder whether we were both so immature that we had no idea how to be in a relationship.

JOHN: Perhaps that was part of it. We have often talked about the fact that you and I were so different and came from such different backgrounds. In some ways, that enriched the relationship. But perhaps it's made it all the more difficult to find common ground and to anticipate issues before they arise and get out of hand. Criticism is a serious issue, I daresay, for most people. We should try to find ways of dealing with it and rendering it constructive rather than destructive. Even the most legitimate criticism, given or taken wrongly, can quickly become destructive.

DIANE: How would you pose the question to a couple considering a long-term relationship? One question within a series of questions about what they anticipate the relationship might be?

JOHN: I think my question would be, "As you grew up in your family, what role did criticism play, and how do you recall dealing with criticism, from parents, siblings, and friends?"

DIANE: And "How did it affect you?"

JOHN: And "What was your emotional response to criticism, as well as the more rational response?"

DIANE: But here we must go back to therapy. I realize that without it, you and I might not have been able to look at criticism rationally, and understand how difficult it was.

JOHN: Certainly, for me, therapy provided a valuable experience with respect to criticism. I discovered that others were just as frail as I, deep down underneath. They had comparable difficulties in dealing with criticism, although, as articulate, sophisticated, well-educated people, they were skillful at putting on the mask and *pretending* that the criticism could be dealt with easily and readily, and that it didn't have an emotional impact, when it really did.

DIANE: Well, in a marriage, or when two people are living together, criticism causes people to knock heads, which is what you and I did for too long.

JOHN: For too long, I certainly agree. And, as you properly noted, the issue is still with us and will always be with us. The lesson is to manage and contain it, and I think we've made some progress in doing so more frequently. I know that I can now, to a much greater degree, hear criticism from you, take a deep breath, and step back and treat it as a comment about a specific issue, and restrict my reaction to that issue.

# Terms of Marital Agreement

The following undertakings are made until October 1, 1982, at which time this marital agreement will be reconsidered anew, without any prior commitments having been assumed by either party.

1. I will be totally uncritical of my spouse. I will not utter a single critical word. I will allow myself to experience how that feels.
2. I will discuss major monetary expenditures as objectively and dispassionately as possible, realizing the particularly heavy demands that will be made on the family budget this fall and winter.
3. I will exercise my freedom to express my sexual feelings honestly. My spouse is not obligated to respond to my sexual advances. I will neither be critical of, nor angry at, my spouse for lack of willingness to make love. I will take responsibility for my own sexual needs.
4. I will exercise my freedom to refuse or accept social invitations. I will not commit us as a couple to any invitation until I have discussed it with my spouse. The refusal or acceptance of one does not necessarily bind the other.
5. I will exercise my freedom to spend time with my friends, male and female. I will be open and honest about my activities. I agree not to engage in any genital sexual activity with any of those friends.

6. I will exercise my freedom to come home in the evenings during the week or not. On weekends, I will honestly discuss my own desires and will exercise my freedom to spend time alone if I choose. I will discuss my needs and intentions in these regards with my spouse.

7. I will exercise my freedom to sleep in a separate room. I will discuss with my spouse my needs and intentions.

8. I will exercise my freedom to attend or stay home from church. My spouse agrees not to pressure me to do otherwise.

9. I will exercise my freedom to suggest, or be open to suggestion, in regard to recreational activities. This might be a movie, a concert, an art gallery, or any other form of recreation that appeals to each of us. From time to time, I will exercise my freedom to engage in recreational activities by myself. I will discuss my needs and my intentions with my spouse. I will take responsibility for my own desires regarding recreation.

10. I will do my best to be loving and kind, warm and affectionate. I understand that the needs of my spouse deserve as much consideration as my own.

11. I will participate in two joint meetings in September with Maxine Denham, to talk with her about our struggles to keep our marriage alive and healthy.

John B. Rehm          Diane A. Rehm

# Psychotherapy

## John

I have been in psychotherapy—or therapy for short—over a number of years. My therapists have been both men and women, and the therapy has been conducted in individual as well as group sessions. It has played a significant role in my life, altering my relationship with myself and with others—especially Diane. Its impact, however, has not always been benign, and at times it has released distinctly ambivalent forces. On the one hand, it has promoted a better understanding of myself. On the other, it has proven divisive and harmful to our marriage.

How have I experienced therapy? For me it is, first and foremost, a process. That is, it is not a set of behavioral rules designed to make me a well-adjusted person. Instead, it creates an affirming environment in which I can see myself more clearly. The therapist and, if it's a group setting, the others demand one thing of me: that I relate my thoughts and experiences with honesty. Such honesty reveals both the good and the bad in me. It can both provoke joy and inflict pain.

My introduction to therapy was bitter. Diane had begun to

work with a female psychotherapist to deal with her own issues, many of which were related to our unhappiness. I remember feeling alarmed that she was seeking help outside the family and thus, I felt, demeaning me. After she refused to allow me to participate in her sessions, I decided, out of a certain degree of desperation, to ask Diane whether I might have a few sessions with the same therapist on my own. During these sessions, the therapist said virtually nothing, and her icy aloofness drove me crazy. Not only was she not helping me, but she provoked in me a hostile and negative reaction. After only two or three sessions, I quit in disgust.

Two years later, Diane began working with a new therapist, this one a female pastoral counselor, an older woman Diane described as warm and kind. I began to envy Diane's relationship with this woman, and, several months later, asked her whether I might occasionally "drop in" on her sessions with the therapist. Understandably, Diane reacted with some annoyance, exclaiming that if I wanted therapy, I'd have to get it on my own time. Diane did, however, introduce me to the pastoral counselor, with whom we each developed, as a couple and as individuals, a long and, for the most part, successful relationship. In particular, although sympathetic, she didn't allow me to dodge the hard questions. For example, what was the true relationship between my father and mother? What needs of Diane's was I not fulfilling? What satisfaction did my absences from my family give me?

Individual therapy with the pastoral counselor enabled me to validate myself. She encouraged me to confront my feelings of insecurity and worthlessness, and at the same time she helped me to understand that, for all my faults, I am lovable. Thus, possessed of greater self-esteem, I was somewhat better able to respond to Diane's needs. At times, however, the therapist's affirmation and acceptance of me led me to believe that Diane—and not I—was the greater cause of our problems.

In group therapy, whether attended by just men or men and women, I was repeatedly struck by one revelation. However educated and sophisticated, each confessed to feelings of remaining a frightened and lonely child. This revelation freed me to attempt to discuss with Diane our mutual problems. However, the temptation to fall back into old and safe patterns of noncommunication remained very strong.

I have learned that, for all its benefits, therapy does create an unreal and potentially deceptive world. By experiencing that world, I've equipped myself to deal with the real world better. But it's vital that I keep the two separate and understand that the relationships created in therapy are only brief exercises that may or may not offer insights that I can apply to my enduring relationships.

# Diane

Therapy has been a lifesaver. It has allowed me, both in group and individual settings, to better understand myself, my behavior, and the impact my behavior has on others. I had always been confident that I had substantial self-knowledge. It wasn't until I got into therapy that I began to realize how little I really understood myself, and how that lack of self-knowledge distorted my view of others.

How did that process begin to work on me, I wonder, and how did I bring that learning into my relationship with John? To start with, John refused to go into joint—or couples—therapy with me. So after long discussions with my friend Jane Dixon, I reluctantly made the decision to go into therapy by myself. For months I resisted the idea that I could in any way benefit from talking our marital problems over with a therapist without having John by my side. They were mostly "his" problems, after all, I kept arguing to Jane, so what good would it do to talk with a therapist alone? Finally, however, she convinced me that the effort would be worthwhile.

Finding the right therapist is not easy, but in my own case, through the help and recommendations of others, I found the right succession of therapists to meet my needs at each juncture. The first time I saw my first therapist, I remember blurting out everything that was wrong with our marriage. Gradually, however, she turned the discussion toward me, my own background, my own expectations of myself, my frustrations, and how I expressed them. She seemed to be less interested in the marriage than I, and each time I tried to return to that subject, she managed to steer me back to my own relationship to myself.

Eventually she urged me to become a part of one of her groups, feeling as she did that group therapy was an opportunity for me to grow more quickly in my self-understanding. Reluctantly I agreed. I say reluctantly because moving into a group seemed less safe and far more threatening than what had become the comfort and familiarity of talking with an individual therapist. But I'm glad I agreed. It was the beginning of a long process, sometimes painful and sometimes filled with joy, laughter, and the satisfaction of sharing my emotions with others who had problems seemingly different from mine.

What the "problems" all came down to, however, were those

of living, coping, and grappling with the realities of our lives, and becoming aware of how the past connected with the present. Each of us had to recognize our unrealistic expectations of others, allow our childhood memories to emerge without backing away from them, and learn to incorporate, without fear, those past experiences into healthy, rational everyday behavior.

But those two years with my first therapist were only the beginning of what has become more than twenty-five years of work with various therapists, male and female. Why should it take so long to straighten out one's thinking? What is the goal of therapy? Is there a moment when I know I'll be finished? I doubt it. For me, the work continues to explore and reveal aspects of my inner life which, at some level, I may have known were there but which were not acknowledged. Now, at sixty-five, I'm ready to let go of the modes of thinking and behavior that for so much of my life controlled me. I believe that I can change the way I actually think. I believe that certain patterns of thinking became repetitious and deeply ingrained many years ago. Now the challenge is to undo the negative ways of thinking and to replace them with altered patterns. I have, among other forms of therapy, experienced cognitive behavioral therapy (CBT), a form of treatment that focuses not on the past but on current ways of thinking, and seeks to put a stop to the old ways, replacing them with the new. In addition to psychotherapy (what most of us would call the "talking therapy"), CBT has been enormously useful in training my mind to work in new ways. Not only where John and I are concerned, but in other difficult personal situations, I have been able to put this new form of thinking to work. Therapy, as I've said, has been a lifesaver.

# Dialogue on Psychotherapy

JOHN: Diane, several times during these conversations you've suggested ways of rendering people somewhat less unprepared for marriage. You've talked about questionnaires, you've talked about marital counseling. It just struck me that therapy is really a way to make up for the absence of such premarriage techniques. That might lead someone to think it's an either-or proposition, that you can make preparations before marriage, or, with the lack of preparation, rely on therapy after the marriage has begun. I'm beginning to think it's a matter of doing both, if at all possible. There's one great advantage of postmarriage therapy. It's that people have a basis of experience—good or bad—to deal with. If it's before marriage, I'm not sure they will have the insight into the problems that will arise.

DIANE: I've talked with some people who've said, "What in the world do you need therapy for? What do you get out of therapy?" First of all, I do agree with you. I don't think that premarital counseling is a substitute for psychotherapy. I think the two are very different. Premarital counseling would just begin to raise the issues that the two people will have to grapple with, or simply raise their awareness of where they'll differ or be similar. Psychotherapy is a learning process in which you come to understand your individual self. Couples therapy perhaps has to come after individual therapy. I don't think you and I could have done the work in couples therapy if each of us hadn't had some work in individual therapy first.

JOHN: Are you suggesting that all couples should anticipate the need for, and undergo, therapy, which can be expensive and time-consuming, and which can also, at times, create wrenches in the relationship? Are we seriously saying you probably can't achieve and manage a successful relationship unless you have a pretty heavy dose of therapy, individual and group?

DIANE: If you've had a perfect childhood, then perhaps you don't need it. But I think there are few perfect childhoods—or marriages. I think most people can be helped, to some extent, by therapy. I agree it's expensive—there's the question of insurance and who pays—but I would also refer to the fifty percent divorce rate in this country. Just think of *that* expense, both financially and emotionally. Perhaps part of that high divorce rate is because two people don't know themselves very well, either before or after they're married, or don't understand their own behavior or that of their partner.

JOHN: Don't you think many couples would say, "Well, we've had our problems, but we've been able to get through them. Those problems really don't go to the heart of our relationship, which is adequate or better. What can I really learn from therapy that I don't already know now?"

DIANE: I was thinking of personality types. You and I both have strong personalities. Maybe there are people out there with calmer approaches to life. And I was thinking of two couples in particular, who seemed to have a benign and quiet relationship, who seemed to exist together as couples very happily, and what happened? Both couples split, after decades of marriage. I don't really know what makes a marriage work, but I do believe that self-knowledge is a must.

JOHN: Maybe it's also a question of just how high your expectations are for marriage. In spite of all of our, at times, severe difficulties, I think you and I, somewhat quixotically, have held on to rather high expectations and a genuine desire for a rewarding, enriching relationship. Maybe that's an unrealistic standard to impose on others.

DIANE: I'm not imposing it on anyone. All I'm suggesting—

JOHN: But you seem to be suggesting that most marriages really need therapy.

DIANE: I'm suggesting that people need to know themselves, and most people don't, and certainly don't fully know their partner.

JOHN: Based on my experience, I would fully agree. But I don't want to mislead people by suggesting that therapy is a sine qua non. That's what I'm probing here. In our case, I would be the first to say it was enormously important. The marriage might not have stayed together if not for the therapy you and I have had. But how seriously are we saying to others, "Gee, whether you know it or not, fellas, you really need to get therapy"?

DIANE: I don't think I'm saying that. I had friends to whom I could talk. You had no one to whom you *would* talk about what was happening in our marriage. I think you were not used to talking with anyone, including me. So how was I to break this impasse to get through to you—I just didn't have a clue. I needed outside help. Many people may not need that kind of help. I needed it. Let's also not forget that many plays and novels have been written about the "quiet desperation" in marriage, and how people simply exist within marriage and don't fully develop themselves. I think you and I have had an opportunity, through therapy, to engage in the process of developing ourselves, and we're still growing.

JOHN: I agree. That has been the enormous benefit of therapy for us. It has allowed us in almost mysterious ways to develop a potential we had for a more successful, rewarding, enriching marriage. I would probably round out this thought by saying that therapy is a resource and can be enlightening. If people are behaving in the belief that ignorance is bliss, and that there is no need to delve into themselves or their partners in order to get along, then so be it. That's not necessarily an unreasonable choice. But if you are trying to deepen and enrich a relationship, then without a doubt therapy can play a role.

DIANE: Now let's talk about the downside of therapy, which for me has been quite similar to the *up*side, in that it's raised issues that I would prefer not to have looked at. It's raised conflicts between you and me. As each of us became stronger in our own views of ourselves, it has, at times, made it that much more difficult for us to come together.

JOHN: Therapy is decidedly ambivalent in the following sense: On the one hand, it can make you confront yourself, your childhood, your behavior, and that can be rough at times. But on the other hand, group therapy, in particular, establishes a cocoon, a protected, sheltered climate, in which the other members of your group are trying to uphold you and show affection for you. In my case, there were times when that was a better world than the one I was experiencing with you. Ultimately, the lessons I learned were constructive rather than destructive, but I can recall being drawn into the weekly session, anticipating a degree of security and a lack of the kind of criticism to which I thought I'd be exposed at home.

DIANE: So the kind of criticism you got there was different from what you got at home, or anticipated you might get, and rendered in a more loving atmosphere. You looked forward to being involved in the group therapy rather than being involved in the real world. It became something of a competition, between what was happening in the safety and security of that group and what was happening at home.

JOHN: I can recall, at times, feeling an emotional bond with individuals in that group. It was really an illusion to believe it could be perpetuated, when, of course, that wasn't the case, because the group would eventually break up and I would return to the "real world." So therapy does have its pitfalls.

DIANE: Yes, it's not all steady growth. There are sharp ups and downs. There are times when you think, I've got to get out of here. This is making my relationship with my partner even *worse*. So it's not simply a straight line upward. But even now, therapy has its long-term rewards that you and I continue to reap, even as we strive, in this forty-second year of our marriage, to enhance the relationship even more.

JOHN: I do agree.

# Retirement

## John

In January 2001 I retired after forty-five years of practicing law, both in and out of the government. During almost all of those years, I specialized in international trade and served the cause of liberalizing commerce among nations. I have consistently believed that nations that trade with each other are less likely to wage war against each other. Protectionism is politically appealing in the short run and economically destructive in the long run.

I had, however, grown tired of practicing law, especially since the profession increasingly suffers from two related trends that I deplore. The first is to judge a lawyer not by qualitative but by quantitative criteria, especially the number of his or her billable hours. The second is to assess a law firm in terms of the bottom line—that is, the amount of profit rather than the extent of service. I was therefore ready for retirement. The question was, how successfully would I manage it.

Looking back over my first year of retirement, I feel good

about what I've done. I believe that I've been responsive to my hopes and sensitive to Diane's feelings. It was my hope to engage in volunteer activities that would take advantage of my talents and allow me to reach out to others. In three areas, I've done so—that is, serving as a docent at the Freer and Sackler museums of Asian art, reading for the blind and dyslexic, and assisting patients at the Hospice of Washington. In each case, I had looked into each program before retiring and had taken the appropriate steps to qualify as a volunteer.

Diane's feelings have been, I think, mixed. I have no doubt that she strongly supported my decision to retire. Moreover, she applauded my choices of volunteer activities. At the same time, she has been somewhat apprehensive about how my new routine would affect our relationship. For example, she's not thrilled by the fact that on some occasions she leaves the house while I'm still asleep, and returns while I'm taking a late afternoon nap. She's also uneasy about her inability to reach me during the day, since I am in and out of public buildings. Previously she could get in touch with me (or my secretary) by phone at the office. Now, because I don't care to carry a cell phone, I am largely out of touch.

More generally, Diane and I are both continuing to adjust to my new way of life. We're asking similar questions: Will my newfound freedom bring us closer? How, if at all, will my experience with the dying at the hospice affect me and our relationship? What steps will we take to establish a new division of household chores, given my increased number of free hours?

Whatever the answers to these questions, it's clear that my retirement is having, and will continue to have, an impact on our relationship. I hope that, as we're doing in other respects, we can talk our way through the difficulties as they present themselves. In this way, my retirement may prove enriching for both of us.

# Diane

After forty-five years of practicing law, John retired at age seventy-one. He has looked forward to, and planned carefully for, this period of his life, choosing activities he wanted to devote time to and training for those activities. There are many benefits, of course. Now he can sleep later in the morning, no longer facing that excruciating sound of an alarm at 5:30 or 6:00 a.m. He can plan his day around the activities he chooses, conducting art gallery tours, visiting museums, going to church, stopping in for noonday concerts, and best of all, he can use time exactly as he pleases. I'm glad for him. I'm, at times, even envious of him, though I myself am not ready to retire yet.

However, as I walked in the door at 6:00 p.m. this evening, after rising at 5:30 a.m., and being at the office since 8:30 this morning, I found a certain irritation arising in me. I heard music coming from the upstairs bedroom, which immediately informed me that John was lying on our bed, asleep, as the music he loved was playing in the background. These late afternoon naps have become a regular part of his daily schedule since his retirement, and I find myself somewhat annoyed by the practice. After all, I'm thinking to myself, he has all afternoon to nap. Why is he napping around the time when I'm coming home? Why can't he have an earlier nap, and then be refreshed and welcoming when I come home?

He awakens, of course, when I walk into the bedroom, and I hug and kiss him. But he's not really interested in talking, because he's still between that beautiful gray dreamworld of sleep, enjoying the solitude he so adores, and the reality of the intrusion of another human being. I ask him a question about his lunch today with his law partner of more than thirty years, and he responds, "I'll tell you all about it." Meaning, "We can talk about it at dinner." Why, I think to myself, can't he tell me all about it now, rather than later? Why do we have to save a snippet of conversation? Is it that he's too sleepy? Or is it part of his desire to control even the timing of our conversations? It will be interesting to talk with him about this, to see what his reaction will be to my observation, indeed, my complaint.

# Dialogue on Retirement

JOHN: When I retired, I think I avoided the trap into which a newly retired person can fall. I really planned ahead and laid out a full regime to occupy my time with pleasure. I know intelligent, thoughtful individuals who've not looked ahead, simply assuming that, after retirement, things would fall into place, that they'd find things to do and create interesting, rewarding days. It's just not that easy, and looking back, I'm rather pleased. First of all, you and I talked about this at length. Second, I've laid out a program of volunteer activities that have proven to be rewarding and enriching, and, I think, of interest to both of us.

DIANE: I'm glad that you've done a lot of planning, because I do think that was key. You thought about this for two years before you retired. You said you'd apply for a docent position at the Freer and Sackler museums, and, in fact, went through a yearlong program of study for that. Now you're engaged in those activities, and they excite you, and that's what pleases me so. There's excitement in your voice. Our son said he'd never seen you so happy. So I think what you're doing is not only making you happy, you're exuding that happiness and sharing it with others around you. As I talk about my own retirement, whenever that may be, David has said to me, "Mom, Dad planned for a long time before he retired. I'd like to see you do the same kind of planning." Of course, as yet, I'm not there. At some point I will be.

JOHN: That raises the second point I wanted to discuss, which I'll call "an imbalance of regimes," which we are now facing, because you are still working, and very busily. These imbalances, I think, have been annoying and even irritating. Just one obvious example: I often get up considerably later than you. You may get up at five-thirty or six in the morning, while I may get up at seven-thirty. Or I may even still be in bed as you leave the house. In the afternoon, I may take a nap, and when you've come home, I'm still sleeping. I can understand how that might create a funny feeling, with no one coming to the door to greet you. These are interim problems, because I think a different set will arise when you retire. I think we're coping with the imbalances, but I know I don't feel totally comfortable yet in my new regime vis-à-vis your current regime.

DIANE: Why don't you feel comfortable with *my* regime? We've talked about why *I* don't feel comfortable, but why don't you?

JOHN: I meant to say that I'm still uncomfortable with *mine,* insofar as it may not mesh with yours.

DIANE: I'm still involved and excited about the day-to-day happenings in the world, because, after all, that's my work. You have an opportunity to read the papers more carefully than I in the morning, because I have to dash off. At the same time, we still have lots to share and talk about, since, in our different ways, we're still *involved* with the world. What scares me is the idea of *my* retiring and turning full time to the garden or leisure. I can't see myself doing that.

JOHN: You mean not keeping up with the world? No, I can't see you doing that. It's not a fear I have.

DIANE: No, I don't think so either.

JOHN: Take the simple question: Once you retire, do we share three meals a day?

DIANE: Somehow I doubt it. Perhaps two, but not three.

JOHN: I think you're right, but that could be a challenge we'll face. But I want to revert for a moment to our present situation and the theme of imbalance. I'm now free to go to a movie in the afternoon alone, but I must confess I'd feel guilty doing so, and especially if the movie was a good one. If it was, the question would be whether it was good enough to see twice, this time with you. That's the kind of issue I'm still wrestling with in terms of what I call the imbalance of regimes.

DIANE: Are you saying that you'd like it if, from time to time, I could take off from the office and join you for a movie in the afternoon?

JOHN: Yes. I guess I'd like to see *my* leisure induce you to set aside a bit more time, particularly as you approach retirement. As you know, in my law firm I began to scale back, I passed clients off to my partners, making it easier for me to move toward retirement. I'd like to see you begin to ease down, instead of making an abrupt shift from a full day to a total nonengagement in your profession.

DIANE: I do think that's conceivable. When I set the date for my retirement, it will be necessary for the station to try out various people over a period of time. For example, I might work four days a week so we'd have an opportunity to try a new host one day a week. I know you've been encouraging me to do that for years. It's not something I want to do *quite* yet, but I'm getting there.

JOHN: I just hope you'll give yourself a lot of lead time. As I found out, even as you reduce the time at the office, you've got to be setting the machinery for retirement in place well beforehand.

DIANE: I'd like to get back to emotions, and the emotional changes I perceive in you as a result of your retirement. I do see you as a happier person—lighter and easier. When you said you were going to retire, of course I was frightened because I've seen so many people get lost. I was frightened for you and for me. You've had a history of separation and withdrawal. I feared retirement might create in you that much more of a desire to retreat. Somehow what's happened has been almost the opposite.

JOHN: I consciously chose three volunteer activities that involve other people. Indeed, they require me to reach out and give them something, whether it's comfort at the hospice or the ability to hear a book when I read for the blind and dyslexic, or a tour of the Freer and Sackler museums. In all those cases, I'm reaching out and connecting with other people. That's been a healthy shift for me.

DIANE: Don't you think it's interesting that you chose those three kinds of activities when, as you've described yourself in this book, you really have been a solitary person? Once again, this seems to be going against your own grain.

JOHN: Going against my grain in some respects. But the desire to help others in a modest fashion has been with me for some time, perhaps since I attended Friends Seminary in New York City. As you know, one of my discomforts about private practice these days is that clients are almost always corporations. You don't deal with individuals and their own problems and situations. That really began to weigh on me and reinforced my determination to engage in activities that involve and benefit other people. I can do that so much more easily now that I'm no longer beset by people at the office—clients, partners, or associates. The choice of people to work with was in my profession largely involuntary. It's now voluntary, which means I work only with those I choose, without resentment and indeed with pleasure.

DIANE: I'm struck by how we seem to be changing places with respect to our attitudes toward retirement. In your activities, you're engaging directly with people. As I contemplate my retirement, I'm thinking more of solitary pursuits, like gardening, painting, and writing. At the same time, I wonder whether your engagement and involvement with other

people has changed or begun to change your relationship
with me here at home.

JOHN: Yes—and perhaps you've already put your finger on it—
it's made me a happier person. Being a happier person does
spill over into our relationship.

# The Other Partner
# as Professional

## John

A successful marriage is one that affirms the several roles that each spouse plays, both in and outside the home. Traditionally, the male spouse was husband, father, and breadwinner. The female spouse was wife, mother, and homemaker. Ideally, our culture expected the husband and wife to respect and honor each other's roles. In recent years, this symmetrical model has been changed by the wife's entry into the workplace. More than fifty percent of married women are now pursuing careers. In most relationships, therefore, the husband and wife must create a new model for integrating their roles to the satisfaction of both.

For the first thirteen years of our marriage, I was the sole breadwinner, trying to straddle my familial and professional worlds. Diane's roles, on the other hand, were pursued strictly within the home. By virtue of my relatively senior legal position in the government, I was known in Washington circles. At social functions, Diane was seen as Mrs. John Rehm and not Diane Rehm in her own right. I was content with this perception, and assumed it would never change. And it didn't during the years when Diane was a volunteer at WAMU-FM. Society considered that role to be ancillary to her primary responsibility for the family. The seeds of change were sown in 1974, when she became a part-time producer of *The Home Show* at WAMU-FM. For some time thereafter, I felt and expressed deep pride in her growing accomplishments as a radio producer and, soon thereafter, a broadcaster. Pygmalion-like, I thought that I had played a role in giving life to her intellectual curiosity.

As the years passed, Diane became a recognized professional, first locally and then nationally. Meanwhile, no longer in the government, I was just one of many highly competent but little-known lawyers in Washington, D.C. Diane's burgeoning success first aroused in me a vague unease. Initially I dispelled that feeling by clinging to the fact that I was still the primary breadwinner. But unease then sharpened into troubling envy, which I tried to contain by drawing away from Diane. At this point Pygmalion's creation had gotten out of hand.

Ultimately, Diane's professional achievements forced me to confront the issue of my own self-esteem. Since graduating from college, I have suffered from fluctuating self-esteem—an at times feeble, and at other times robust, confidence and satisfaction in myself. In my experience, true self-esteem can't rest upon the flattery of others, nor can it be created by a recitation of good works. Instead, it arises from an elusive sense of wholeness, which allows me to accept my fears and exploit my strengths.

For some time I've felt—though didn't admit—that the

degree of my self-esteem was in inverse proportion to the level of Diane's success. That is, the greater the recognition of her career, the lesser the value of my work. It was not that I envied Diane in her profession, since I had no desire to be a radio broadcaster. But Diane was upsetting the paradigm to which I was perhaps unconsciously clinging—that is, that the husband/father is the head of the household in the eyes of his family and community. This paradigm, of course, was prevalent during the early years of our marriage, and is viewed differently by today's younger generation.

It took me some time to come to grips with the fact that Diane's success did not have to diminish me. I had to disentangle myself from her activities and allow the value of my work to be assessed on its own merits. In this light, I feel good about the work that I have done, in and out of the government, to promote the liberalization of trade among nations. But even apart from Diane, my self-esteem remains vulnerable to nagging doubts.

With a generosity of spirit, Diane credits me with opening the door to her professional future. I credit Diane with seizing the opportunities as they came along. In this sense, we have shared in the creation and growth of her now international program.

# Diane

I knew from the beginning of our relationship that John was serious about his professional life, and I totally supported his drive to succeed. I understood that what he did as an attorney for the government and in private practice was not only in his best interest but in our family's as well. What I didn't realize was exactly what that would mean: long hours away from home, putting job before family. For more than a dozen years, he couldn't deal with the separate demands of wife, young children, and profession all at the same time.

Of course I was immensely proud of him, and knew how highly his colleagues regarded him. I also knew just how important the work he was doing really was. How did I know? Because, on those rare occasions when we could go to a social gathering together, his coworkers, and even his superiors, told me so. Therefore, despite my loneliness, it was hard for me to voice any complaints to them.

I made friends with other wives whose husbands worked in the field of international trade, most of them older than I, but none with small children. While it was good to be in touch with other women and to know that their husbands were working similarly arduous schedules, I was not particularly comforted. I thought I was the only one with justifiable complaints. I felt sorry for myself, and I took my resentment out on John, making his day-to-day tasks that much more difficult.

During the Kennedy-Johnson era, John had risen to the senior position of general counsel to the U.S. Special Trade Representative, Governor Christian Herter. John regards his years in government as the most satisfying of his professional life, and I can understand why. However, I also recall them as the most difficult for our family. It was during those years that we got into a terrible pattern. He would work and work, and by the time he came home, I was so angry I wasn't even glad to see him. I complained. I whined. I cried. I screamed. He withdrew. It was a pattern that lasted for perhaps his entire tenure in government, with only short breaks for vacations at the beach or at the farm. Even those could not be considered sacrosanct. There were several occasions when we arrived either at the farm or at the beach only to learn that John had to leave to respond to clients' needs. The children were enormously disappointed, and I was livid, enraged that our only period for a joint family vacation had been taken from us.

I must confess that I also resented the fact that I, as John's wife, was not perceived by society at that time as a fully contributing partner to the family unit, since I earned no income. Perhaps unrealistically, I saw myself as a coequal, raising our children and caring for our home while he took on the more public aspect of our joint venture. But as at social gatherings all over the world, when the inevitable question of "What do you do?" came up, I was annoyed to note a total lack of interest if I identified myself as a homemaker. Someday I hope this country will recognize the important contributions of stay-at-home mothers to our society. It's as though, on the one hand, we stress the importance of raising healthy children and creating a stable home life for them, while on the other hand we fail to acknowledge those contributions in the form of tax credits or even credits toward social security.

With Richard Nixon's election, John left government and joined a law firm. He went through a rocky time professionally, doubting himself and his ability to perform in the private sector. It was another difficult period for us, since he brought those doubts home with him in the form of depression and withdrawal. There was additional income, but that didn't begin to compensate for the new tensions. What did serve as compensation, however, was our widening circle of friends, beginning with John's partner, David Busby, and his wife, Mary Beth.

John's professional life, from my perspective, has been successful and rewarding for both of us. While he worked in the public and private sectors, I was free to develop my own interests in several areas, including cooking, sewing, playing the piano, and gardening. I wouldn't have been able to move into my own career as a broadcaster had it not been for the income he earned throughout those years, which allowed me the freedom to become a nonpaid worker and to pursue a vocation of my own. I have loved the relationships that have been created through his working life. Those are friends who will be ours for a lifetime.

John has provided a secure home for our family, permitted our children to receive fine educations, and created a nest egg for us to go forward into retirement. For that I'll always be grateful, as I am for having journeyed with him through the evolution of his extraordinary professional life. I only wish we had found ways to openly discuss, in rational terms, our frustrations, instead of hiding behind anger and fear. I wish I had been a more mature and understanding wife, recognizing that there were constructive ways to deal with my anger and disappointments, and that tirades were counterproductive. We got through those years, but only by the skin of our teeth.

# Dialogue on the Other Partner's Profession

DIANE: First of all, I want to say how fortunate we've both been in terms of our professional lives. Perhaps I've been more fortunate than you, in that I've enjoyed my professional life in its entirety somewhat more than you because I chose it without choosing. It just happened. You chose professionally to use your talents as a gifted lawyer in the Kennedy and Johnson administrations, doing work you loved. After that, I think your love of work diminished considerably, and with that diminishment came even greater difficulty in our marriage.

JOHN: I think that's true, and it just struck me why I did become envious of your success as a radio broadcaster. I think it's because you did enjoy it so thoroughly, while I, as you know, had reservations about private practice and the value of my work. I was representing my clients with a high degree of competence, that was clear, but I never had the kind of satisfaction that I did in government, promoting the commonweal. Yes, to help corporations solve their problems did contribute to the economic vitality of the country and did have value. But it didn't provide anything near the satisfaction of what I did in the government, and in two programs in particular: foreign aid and trade liberalization.

DIANE: So what could we have done to make things happier for both of us? I couldn't do anything to make your life happier. You seemed to be an unhappy person in the midst of lucrative and productive work. I must say I was flummoxed. I didn't know how to help you. You had such a productive job and were so highly thought of, and you earned the kind of income that you did. Yet there was this core of unhappiness within you that I couldn't seem to do anything about.

JOHN: In some ways, looking back, I wish I had stayed in the government. But once Nixon was elected, I knew that I would be extremely unhappy in that administration. I'm not saying I predicted Watergate, but there was a meanness, a narrowness, a parochial attitude among his senior White House aides with whom I worked briefly that just turned me off. I was an ardent Humphrey supporter, and had he been elected, I might have stayed on, and my career, though less lucrative, would have been more satisfying. As to what you could have done, I can't fault you in any significant way for your behavior. I was wrestling with myself, trying to come to terms with myself, which I did to a degree, but not wholly satisfactorily. Therapy and counseling certainly did help. But I was still wrestling with the basic fact that I was never wholly happy in private practice.

DIANE: You seemed stuck, somehow, in your sense of unhappiness. It was almost going against the grain for you to earn the kind of income you did. I wonder, had I not had the kind of career I've had, would that have made it somewhat easier for you, do you think?

JOHN: No, I don't. One of my great satisfactions is having helped you grow in intellectual terms. I've often said I was Pygmalion and you were Galatea. It was just that Galatea got out of hand.

DIANE: [*laughter*]

JOHN: Your success is certainly well deserved. Insofar as I did and do take genuine pride in your success, that made me feel better. It made me feel that I had made a contribution through you to society, if you will. But at times it did bring on an envy as well. For a while, somehow, the greater your success, in proportionate terms, the more my self-esteem fell. It took me a while to realize that your success didn't have to affect or diminish my self-esteem.

DIANE: People—unthinking, insensitive people—have at times made jokes, referring to you as Mr. Diane Rehm. I always cringe, and have wondered how you've felt about that.

JOHN: At times it annoys me. If I'm not feeling all that good about myself, it has a sting to it and makes me brood a bit more. But I'm reminded of one occasion when I accompanied you on one of your book promotion tours, and that was beneficial. It gave me an indication of just how much your listeners admired and, indeed, loved you. They also made the point that they admired me for supporting you and promoting your career, and that made me feel good.

DIANE: I certainly hope you felt that I did exactly the same for you in your career.

JOHN: I have no doubt of that. That was certainly true. So, on balance, I'm pleased with your success. I've been able to manage it, to adjust to it. And that's been good for our relationship.

DIANE: There's been a lot of use of mood-altering drugs, like Zoloft, Paxil, and Prozac, that are supposed to be useful in treating low self-esteem, depression, and a feeling of being disconnected from the rest of the world. I sometimes asked you whether you felt that any of those drugs might help you. Do you think you—and we—might have benefited by your use of those drugs? Do you think their use in the past five or ten years might have helped?

JOHN: I don't know because I never tried. But from my earliest days I had this conviction that you take life as it comes and deal with it, for better or for worse, without artificial support or means. I would think less of myself if I got through the day relying on one of these drugs.

DIANE: That all sounds very noble.

JOHN: No, it's not noble, but rather a desire that I want to taste life authentically, in terms of my immediate, direct, and unadulterated confrontation with reality.

DIANE: But your confrontation with reality was, in effect, a confrontation with me that didn't make either of our lives happy. So when I ask you what you might have done, it seems as though you stuck your feet in the ground and said, "I'm going to live my life this way. I have a professional life. I don't really like it, but I'm going to live with it, *and* I'm going to take my dissatisfaction with my profession out on you." That's how it felt.

JOHN: I can see that. It wasn't my intention. What I'm aware of is a deep distaste for getting along by artificial means.

DIANE: What would you say to a young man in his thirties going through the same kind of struggle to achieve, to attain self-esteem, to make it through, and at the same time to keep balance in his life?

JOHN: Well, hold on to the relationships you have, including wife and children. That leads me to say that, during this period, I did have a good relationship with David and Jennie. I look back on those years, and think that I was of genuine assistance to them, in terms of love, support, encouragement, sharing some of their problems and difficulties. My relationship with you was far more ambivalent, but we also had some good times. I don't have any great words of wisdom, other than to maximize the pleasures and to carry a sense of gratitude for what you have. I know you don't like relativistic comments, but for all of my problems and difficulties, I've been enormously blessed, as I compare my state with that of billions of disadvantaged people on this earth. So I hope I didn't engage in self-pity.

DIANE: Do you think it was self-pity? Or was it just dissatisfaction with your own professional life?

JOHN: Not self-pity but an undercurrent, which has decreased in recent years, of continuing difficulty with the marital condition itself. I've never been totally persuaded that the kind of a long-term commitment we're talking about is right for me, although, on balance, considering recent years, I have no question that it has been.

DIANE: So looking back over the long haul, your preference would have been not to marry?

JOHN: Part of me feels that way. Not marrying, leading a somewhat nomadic life, like journalism, or teaching without a long-term commitment to an institution, something like my father's life. He was essentially nomadic.

DIANE: Hearing you talk about him and his "nomadic" life, I sense a kind of dreamy quality on your part. Perhaps you'd prefer to have done other things—

JOHN: —a job that would have drawn on my intellectual skills, but wouldn't have committed me to a particular path. I say that, and another voice, immediately in response, says, "Well, that would not have been a satisfactory life. You would have missed being a part of raising two marvelous human beings, and missed a lot of good times with you." It's just that, for me, the equation is a lot closer than it is for you. I think you feel that, by and large, you've had great satisfaction and great success, with fewer regrets than I. I'm not sure of that, but that's my sense.

DIANE: So, for you, the word "commitment" continues to feel somewhat constricting.

JOHN: Yes, but that's now enormously eased by my retirement. The banner of my retirement is freedom. I'm now free to do what I want, in the way of scheduled activities or just to take a long walk, enjoy the sky, the air, the flowers. So many of the pressures that led to a disquietude and dissatisfaction have now to a great degree been lifted. This makes me easier with you, family, friends, and the like.

DIANE: Can you look back on your professional life and marriage and say, "I have been blessed with a good life"?

JOHN: Unquestionably true, particularly as I look about me and see so many people who are fundamentally disadvantaged in so many ways. Yes, absolutely. A life without regrets? No. And how would you answer your own question?

DIANE: If you're asking whether I believe in commitment, the answer is, of course I do. I have grown tremendously as a result of living a life that has challenged me, both personally and professionally. If I hadn't been committed to making this marriage an important part of my essential existence, who knows where I'd be now? The issue is devotion: devotion to partner, to children, to extended family, and to friends. Commitment is something that comes easily to me, even though, as you well know, there have been many times when I would have given up on you and the marriage. But there was always a sense in me that what you and I were building together was important, not just to us but to those around us. We loved together, we created children together, we fought together, and we'll continue to work together. For me, that is the essence of commitment, and commitment is at the center of my life.

# Holiday Celebrations

## John

Despite many years of celebrating family holidays, such occasions continue both to reward and to disappoint us. We anticipate them by combining memories and hopes. The memories preserve the vividness of happy, though fleeting, moments. The hopes obscure the disappointments of past celebrations; they create the illusion of a perfect celebration. As a result, we approach holidays with unrealistic expectations, along with feelings of vulnerability.

I have found Christmas to be the most problematic holiday, with distinctly bright and dark features. However fragile, the bright features are largely defined for me by such activities as shopping, trimming the tree, wrapping and opening presents, cooking, and feasting. In our family, the list also includes the religious component of singing carols and attending a church service. These bright aspects of Christmas should ensure that our celebration will be joyous.

Yet Diane and I experience Christmas as a time not only of

joy but also of melancholy, which arises for several reasons. The very darkness of December creates a gloom that we struggle against, more or less consciously.

Much of the ceremony of Christmas is an effort to dispel that gloom, as with tall candles and chains of light. Moreover, this gloom of December is subtly intensified by the recollection of deaths that occurred around this time. My parents died in the months of October and November, preceding Christmas, and Diane's father and mother died in November and on New Year's Day, respectively. It took me some years to understand the subliminal power of these sad memories. As one of our therapists put it: "The body remembers."

In addition, each year I unwittingly fashion, and fall prey to, an image of the perfect Christmas: at church, the Christmas hymns will all be my favorites, my presents will be uniformly liked, and every element of the Christmas dinner will be praised. Above all, the members of our family will set aside—for the day—all tensions and irritations. In one telling respect or another, however, my image will be tarnished. The season's spirit will flag and then revive, and I will count it—with some disregard of the facts—as another good Christmas.

In recent years I've done a better job of dealing with this threefold melancholy. I accept its presence and don't look to others to allay it. By virtue of that, I'm a little more sensitive to the anxiety others face over Christmas. The close of Christmas typically brings a sigh of relief. I used to think of this as a sign of failure. I now have a better understanding of most of the elements at work, the choices I can make, and how those choices will, in turn, affect not only my own experience of Christmas but that of others as well.

# Diane

I'm a child when it comes to holidays. I want to have all our friends at our home for Easter brunch. I love to see the table filled with people at Thanksgiving. And the tree, the presents, the food at Christmas—I expect all of it to be perfect. Unfortunately, these childhood fantasies rarely come true in adulthood, no more than they do in childhood. I remember the arguments at Thanksgiving, the absence of a hoped-for Easter basket, and the last days of my dying mother in the hospital at Christmas.

There is a part of me that actually dreads holidays. The memories weigh me down, even as I try to put them aside and reach for new experiences. And those long-ago experiences seem to affect my body as well. Time and time again, sometime between the first of November and the end of January, I have become ill. I have gotten a bit better about taking extra care of myself during that period, knowing how vulnerable I am. But I can't seem to get beyond the sad memories of almost fifty years ago, when both my parents died in the same year, she on New Year's Day and he on what was then called Armistice Day. So the holiday spirit begins with sadness, with longing, and with a hunger, perhaps, to share for a moment the company of those no longer here.

For various reasons, holidays are difficult for lots of people I know. Some of the spirit of Christmas, of course, has been lost due to the enormous emphasis on its commercial aspects. We are told again and again what department stores hope to make in the way of sales. It's as if there's some kind of patriotic duty to go out and buy, to keep the economy healthy—the department stores need us! We're reminded every minute on radio and television of the gift choices we can make for friends and relatives. We hear popularized Christmas carols, instead of the traditional arrangements that help create the beautiful sound of the holiday.

As an escape from the overdone store decorations and the constant advertisements, John and I turn to more quiet and peaceful activities. We love going to church and singing hymns of celebration, thanksgiving, and joy, and, at Easter, participating in the service that calls upon the congregation to be the crowd demanding Christ's crucifixion. Being within that church helps me to center myself and focus on our family and friends, those we know who are sick and those who are healthy, as well as the problems of the larger world.

I promise myself each year that I'll do a better job of planning for Christmas, and yet each year I put it off. It's only in the last few years that I've learned to take a few days off to bake special gifts of cake and baklava. Also in the past few years, John has taken a more active role in shopping, wrapping, planning, and generally participating more fully, so that the burden is not totally on me. When Jennie and David were living at home, they both helped out a great deal. Now they must create their own family celebrations, devoid, as much as possible, of the kinds of sadness that have weighed me down, undermining my ability to celebrate these special times of the year.

## Dialogue on Holiday Celebrations

DIANE: For me the last few years of holidays have been somewhat easier, simply by virtue of asking for more help. I cannot do it alone. That's true not only at Christmas but at Easter as well. We used to have a wonderful Easter party, with all of our friends here for brunch. I reached the point where I couldn't do it anymore. You and I have both written about our expectations of these holidays, and at this age I think we just have to let go of these expectations.

JOHN: I fully agree. We think it all has to be perfect, and when it doesn't turn out that way, we whip ourselves. I've learned from you the extent to which you've anticipated holidays like Christmas with some dread. Over time, we've identified a number of reasons for that. But most importantly, if I had had an early sense of that dread I think I might have behaved differently in anticipating holidays like Christmas. I think we would both have been less prone to set up these lofty goals, which almost ensure, by their ambition, that they won't be met.

DIANE: You know, it all starts with our wedding date, which was December 19. Now, how much closer to Christmas can you get? That puts yet another burden on us. I'm not in any way trying to discourage people from getting married around Christmas, because it's a very beautiful time of the year. But that simply has added to our sense of pressure to make the holiday season perfect.

JOHN: I think we've conjoined December 19 with December 25, and expected so much of each. The trick here is, on the one hand, to thoroughly enjoy the anticipation of these events, and at the same time to be far more realistic as to what they can provide.

DIANE: What you and I have finally learned to do is to scale back anticipations, what we can and will accomplish. For example, I used to spend weeks baking and getting everything ready, in addition to carrying on with my full-time job and trying to do all the shopping as well. What I've done in recent years is to take a few days off work before the holidays. I've managed to scale down the baking. You and I have done the shopping together; we've done things more as a team, rather than as in the old days, when all of the responsibility was *mine*.

JOHN: I'm amazed by the extent to which we didn't learn from past experience. I can recall a series of Christmases when you would have to go to *bed* on Christmas night. It almost became a family joke, although there was a good reason for you to go to bed: you were exhausted. We all clustered around the bed and watched movies like *The Sound of Music* or *Willy Wonka & the Chocolate Factory*. The thing that strikes me, as I look back, is how this pattern would continue, year after year. You'd think we'd have recognized the problem and done something about it, but we went on getting caught up in the power of these illusions. It's taken a long time to break that down, without forgoing the pleasure and the joy that do coexist.

DIANE: There were so many Christmases, Thanksgivings, and Easters when, no doubt as a result of that pressure, you and I got into huge arguments, not speaking for weeks and both unwilling to come back together until the day of the holiday itself. There was actually one Easter party we gave at which you didn't show up. It was awful.

JOHN: I guess if there are already tensions in a relationship and you pile a holiday on top of that, yes, it's going to exacerbate those tensions and also make the holiday more problematic.

DIANE: I think of our daughter and her husband. She was raised as an Episcopalian and he is Jewish. Now they need to reach a compromise as to how they'll celebrate the various holidays. When you and I were first married, you had no interest in religion. Your family had minimized the celebrations. When we went up to the farm that very first Christmas to spend our honeymoon there, I think for my sake your mother had decorated the house, and there were a few presents. But you all didn't do very much of that.

JOHN: Well, there was an exchange of gifts, and there was also a holiday dinner, which my parents prepared very well indeed. But if I were talking to a young couple, I would urge them to try to reveal, as much as possible, the darker side of each one's approach to holidays, and to recognize that the anxieties and sad memories are going to have an impact and should be taken into account. I tended to gloss over them, thinking that Christmas shouldn't entail sadness. But it does. A surprising number of people will say, if they're willing to answer the question honestly, "Christmas? I dread Christmas. It's a difficult time, and the best I can do is just to get through it." Well, maybe we could have done better than just "get through it" if we had had a fuller understanding of each partner's true feelings about Christmas, including the sad memories.

DIANE: Perhaps not just the sad memories but also what experiences each grew up with and what each expects. Really talk it through. Going back to the beginning, we never shared our expectations or exchanged what we wanted it to be. I just went ahead and did it. You went along.

JOHN: In some ways, I think we're all victims of Martha Stewart— is that her name?—the Martha Stewart psychology, if I may put it this way. I was recently flipping through her magazine and all the gloriously glossy photographs of everything in perfect place, the colors, the fabrics, and all the rest. That just does a profound disservice to all those who are trying to celebrate holidays and enjoy other occasions. Let's start from a far more realistic base, with lesser expectations and greater cooperation, but fundamentally understand that any holiday is an *im*perfect occasion. It won't achieve perfection, and we don't have to beat ourselves up because it does not.

# Illness

## John

My parents' constitutions largely determined their antagonistic approach to illness—their own and mine. My father was ruggedly healthy. By his own admission, his experience with sickness was limited to a few headaches and stomachaches over his lifetime. He could eat and drink whatever he wanted, and he was unusually impervious to cold. He also had a high threshold of pain, enduring surgery on his shinbone on the strength of a single glass of calvados. My mother, on the other hand, suffered all her life from daily headaches, although she was organically sound. Some days the headaches were tolerable, while on other days they drove her into her bedroom, which had been made as dark and quiet as possible. In one of my earliest childhood memories, I'm placing a cold compress on her forehead. Elsewhere in the apartment in Paris, my father is regaling friends with oysters and white wine.

My father tended to view my mother as a hypochondriac. He did not believe that she was fabricating her headaches, but he couldn't accept their daily presence and offered little sympathy. Robust as he was, he viewed her complaints as exaggerated and self-indulgent. My mother, in turn, considered him intolerant and uncaring.

Out of her own experience, my mother was particularly sensitive to my boyhood illnesses. If I was able to go to school yet still felt a little sick, my mother didn't hesitate to keep me at home. Indeed, at times she would give me what she called "rest cures." These would last for a day or so, and were more preventive than remedial—and quite enjoyable. I would spend most of the time in bed, dozing, reading, or listening to music on the radio. My mother would bring me a tray of favorite foods that I would consume sitting up in bed. My father didn't approve, fearing that I too would become a hypochondriac, but my mother had her way and the rest cures continued. In short, I have happy memories of being ill, and illness still connotes for me warmth and affection.

Diane's experience was unhappily all too different. When she became ill, she was treated in a manner that was tantamount in her mind to punishment. Her mother apparently believed that the best medicine for any sickness was the enema—which Diane hated. Her mother withheld sympathy, making Diane feel that she was somehow responsible for her illness. No wonder that she concealed her sicknesses in order to avoid such maternal abuse.

In our marriage, we have had to reconcile our different approaches to illness. At a time of sickness, I am more likely to listen to the body and give it sympathetic care at home. Diane, on the other hand, is more apt to override what the body is saying, and tough it out at work. When she does decide to stay in bed, I enjoy taking care of her. Her sickness creates an intimacy based on her need for me. I think it took some time for her to accept my sicknesses instead of dismissing them as unworthy of care. In short, I have retained my maternal model, while Diane has had to overcome hers.

In the summer of 1988, I suffered a pinched sciatic nerve, which brought on excruciating pain and prevented me from walking. My doctor recommended surgery, but I decided to lie in bed for four weeks, hoping that such prolonged rest would induce the body to heal itself. As a result, Diane became responsible for feeding me breakfast, lunch, and dinner in bed. Instead of returning at noon, she left me with a delicious cold lunch. Also, she asked our close friends to help out by occasionally bringing around dishes for me at lunch. Diane certainly had doubts—as I did—about the value of my regime (which failed and led to my agreeing to surgery, which turned out to be successful), but she was able to disengage herself from her childhood and care for me in a loving way.

# Diane

I like to think of myself as a healthy person. Anyone looking at me would surely think I was one. I am slim. My skin color is good. I exercise. I do not smoke. I drink lots of water, eat a mixture of fresh foods, and take a few supplemental vitamins. So what has long troubled me is why I get ill as frequently as I do, and why, in some cases, my illnesses last as long as they do.

When I was a child, I tried at all costs to avoid the appearance of illness. I dreaded missing the pleasure of being with teachers and playing with friends at school. And I hated having to endure the sickness regime my mother imposed, which included lots of enemas, Milk of Magnesia, and other less than pleasant medications. The only things I looked forward to were the chance to lie in bed listening to the radio, and the delicious homemade chicken soup she made, with a sprinkle of cinnamon added. I can still smell the aroma.

Looking back on our marriage, I realize I've had a fair amount of illness, including various colds and viruses, pneumonia, stomach problems, headaches, backaches, and the aftermath of surgery. Along with those memories comes the realization that throughout it all, John has been there to care for me. I don't mean just checking in to see how I am, but caring for me in the fullest sense of the word.

I shall never forget how stunned we were when, in the early months of my first pregnancy, there were some signals that I might miscarry. My obstetrician didn't believe in using medications to save the pregnancy, such as diethylstilbestrol (DES), which later was found to cause testicular and ovarian cancers in the children of mothers who received the drug. Instead, he advised complete bed rest for at least ten days. At the time, we were living in a house in Georgetown belonging to John's aunt. So John made breakfast for me each day before he left for the State Department, then returned at noontime to prepare a nourishing lunch. After work, he made our dinner. I barely had to leave the bed. A healthy baby boy emerged, I believe, as a result of John's care.

John's experience of illness was so different from mine. His mother was especially attentive to him whenever he was sick. She read to him to encourage him to eat when he had no appetite, and spent time with him when he needed company. She allowed him to take what she called "rest cures," when he could miss school to stay in bed for a slight cold. I think she really believed that the best way to cure illness in her son was to coddle him, and apparently it worked.

There came a time during the Second World War when she had to undergo an operation, while John's father was off in Europe. It was John who nursed her and cared for her during her recuperation. What John brought to our marriage was that very same approach, one I'll always be grateful for. He taught me that I needn't be afraid of illness or try to hide it, as I had done for so much of my life. In turn, he gave me the model by which I could care for our children, trying to be as comforting to them during their childhood illnesses and injuries as he was to me. Eventually I became more aware of my attitudes to illness and was able to put most of my fears behind me.

So, back to the question of why I get sick as frequently as I do. Perhaps, without my being consciously aware of it, illness has been a way for me to reach out and ask for help, for caring and kindness, when I perceived that things were difficult between John and me. Maybe the only way I "knew"—without knowing—how to connect with him was to get sick. I'm not suggesting that I took unnecessary risks or foolishly exposed myself to extreme temperatures or weather conditions. What I'm suggesting is that the well-being of the body can be vulnerable to the heart's needs. When I've felt an emotional void between us, perhaps my body has felt sufficiently wounded to respond with illness. It's remarkable to observe this interaction of mind and body, a connection I've long believed in.

Now I come to the issue of spasmodic dysphonia (SD), with which I was diagnosed several years ago. SD is a neurological disorder affecting the vocal cords, leading to excessive and inappropriate contractions of the cords when an individual tries to speak. My type is called adductor SD, and produces a cracked and broken voice.

For years I knew something was wrong with my voice. I would find myself choking or growing hoarse, unable to complete a sentence. I consulted many physicians and specialists, all in vain. I could hear the difficulty, and it was getting worse. I knew I couldn't keep going, and I took myself off the air.

I spent four months at home, sitting quietly, reading, meditating, and trying to stay away from the phone and all other vocal contact with people except for the therapists who helped me get through this period. Here I cannot say enough for John's support and caring. We discussed all the various possibilities, including my leaving the air, but he encouraged me each day not to give up, believing that ultimately there would be some answer to this mysterious ailment.

Finally, at the insistence of my internist, Dr. Carole Horn, I went to the Johns Hopkins University Medical Center. There, neurologist Stephen Reich and otolaryngologist Paul Flint concluded that I had SD. It was such a relief at last to know what was wrong with me and that something could be done.

There is no known cause for SD. Neither is there a cure. There are, however, various treatments, and I chose periodic injections of botulinum toxin (Botox), plus weekly acupuncture sessions and various medications prescribed by my physicians. When I have injections of Botox (every five to six months), I must be off the air for several days, waiting for the vocal cords to resume their normal vibration.

In a curious way, I believe illness is an area where John and I have strengthened the bond between us. Both of us have exhibited, without reservation, the greatest kindness, caring, and respect for each other when we are under the weather. When John is not feeling well, he usually asks for quiet in our darkened bedroom. He sleeps until he feels better, demanding very little, even in the way of food. When I am sick in bed, the more sunlight the better, and I'm always hungry. Even with those differences, we seem to have handled each other's attitude toward illness and the experience of it quite well.

"In sickness and in health," goes that familiar phrase from the wedding vow. It is a promise that, despite all of our other problems, John and I have kept well.

# Dialogue on Illness

JOHN: In approaching the issue of illness, I'm struck by a certain complementarity that you and I have brought to feelings about illness. In my case, based upon a happy experience of illness and the amount of caring my mother showed, I have positive feelings about illness. As you've explained in your essay, your feelings are different. In that sense, I was able to make up for, to remedy, what was a really dark and serious aspect of your childhood feeling about illness. I can recall the pleasure of being needed when you were sick, of being there to take care of you, and I still experience that pleasure.

DIANE: I can't tell you how much I've appreciated that over the years. But, because of our different backgrounds, I think there's not only been a reluctance on my part to accept my own illness but also, to a certain extent, an unwillingness to be sympathetic about your fragile stomach, for example. Your stomach has entered into our relationship a lot. There've been a number of social occasions when you've said, "My stomach just doesn't feel well." I haven't had much sympathy for that kind of mild infirmity. On the other hand, when your back went out and you had to have an operation, I was sympathetic.

JOHN: I think that's true. But one of the things I've had to contend with has been your reluctance not only to accept your body but also to *listen* to your body when it was saying, "I'm really stressed out. I've been overworking. My hours are too long." Typically, your response has been, "Well, I'll tough it out. My body be damned. I will prevail." Of course, you can't always prevail over your body. In turn, that's brought on darker feelings about your body in general.

DIANE: I think you're right. I do resist the feeling of sickness and the need to stay at home, given the kind of job I've had in the past twenty years. It's not easy to call in sick. If I had another kind of employment and was not expected to be at that microphone every day, perhaps I'd feel differently. I have resisted. I can remember one of my therapists telling me that he thought my body would just "shut down" and not be able to take it anymore. On the other hand, I've felt you've given in *too easily* when you've said to yourself, for example, "My stomach hurts so I'll stay home." So I feel you give up too easily, and in contrast, you're impatient because you believe I go on too long.

JOHN: You go on too long, and then, instead of having a series of milder ailments, it reaches a point where you *really* get sick. I can just see you from time to time coming back from the office looking utterly drained, saying, "I'm just exhausted." Then you'll go to bed and be sick for a day or two. Here I'm really criticizing myself, as well as you, because I've done the same thing. If you have a demanding job you enjoy, you really have to adopt a stoic attitude. But that attitude comes back to hurt you—and the relationship.

DIANE: How does it affect the relationship?

JOHN: At times I've had a feeling of more than irritation that you weren't handling your body well, that you were operating at the margin and then allowing your body to collapse. I feel I've been abused in the process, because you're thinking of yourself and your job and the need for you to be at the office. But I have to deal with the aftermath, when I'm supposed to be there to take care of you.

DIANE: I accept that. I think you're raising a good point. We've been dealing in the last few years with a number of debilitating processes that have gone on within my body. I think I'm improving. At the same time, you haven't responded to my worry about what I would term your *excessive* self-concern, such as your reaction to a stomachache, when others might say, "Well, OK, I have a stomachache, but I'll keep going." For me, the opposite is quite true, which is why *I've* gotten impatient and seen our relationship affected. I don't like it when you pull out at the last minute on a social event.

JOHN: I don't think I do that very often, but let me make two points. First, there have certainly been times when I've used not feeling well as an excuse to get out of a social occasion. Second, I don't buy this notion that the slightest stomachache sends me to bed. I won't belabor this, but for long periods, I went to the office day after day with a stomach more or less upset. So I've had to contend with that, and for the most part I think I've done fairly well.

DIANE: I wonder about other couples and the extent to which illness becomes a focus, if not *the* focus, of their relationship. There've been times over these past forty-two years when illness has become a central issue within our relationship and, when serious, has actually brought us closer together.

JOHN: Yes. When you and I have been estranged, illness has come along as a kind of boon to the relationship, and has allowed us to come back together. I do think there's a tendency to treat sickness as "my problem—I'll deal with it *my* way," and not recognize it as something that invariably impinges upon the relationship and can do so quite seriously. I'm not talking about a life-threatening illness but the day-to-day illnesses. They're not the business of just one spouse but of the other as well.

DIANE: And you go back to the marriage vows, "in sickness and in health." I have wondered, from time to time, whether my frustration with you over your separation and isolation has, in fact, worked psychologically to make me ill, knowing full well that you would be there to help me.

JOHN: So it was perhaps a device used to overcome separation?

DIANE: I wouldn't use the word "device," but I think I may have been emotionally wounded to such an extent that I might give in to sickness as opposed to taking care of myself. I would be hoping that you would be there.

JOHN: And in my case, I've enjoyed your being sick and the opportunity for me to assist you in that cozy place where we could shut out the rest of the world and you're just "my Diane."

# Food

## John

Food comes in many guises. It can be nutritious, harmful, soothing, belligerent, sympathetic, and unforgiving. Each of us has a unique approach to food, dating back to childhood. Sooner or later what may seem to be a neutral factor in a marriage will become an issue.

Diane and I each brought to our marriage what is loosely called a "nervous stomach," together with a history of trying to disregard a sensitivity to certain foods. I learned this about Diane early in our courtship. Each morning she would regularly skip breakfast, have a coffee upon arrival at the State Department, and then suffer stomach pains before lunch. I suggested to her that she might avoid such pains if she had a bite to eat before drinking the coffee. I recall being both sympathetic and annoyed with her. During law school, I suffered from an irritated duodenum, which left my stomach intolerant of all but bland foods. I knew how a chronic stomachache could distort your outlook on life. At the same time, I was aghast that an intelligent adult could so willfully and repeatedly harm herself. Surely she must have known that coffee is hard on an empty stomach.

Diane and I both understand and accept admonitions like "Listen to your body," "Be good to your stomach," and "Avoid those foods you know will upset you." For the most part, our diet is wholesome and nutritious and we happily don't suffer from obesity or any other food-related affliction. We're happy that, in this regard, our children have followed in our footsteps. The fact remains, however, that food is problematic for me. At times it's the source of hypocritical and even divisive behavior. I am drawn, in particular, to several kinds of food that I know will upset my stomach and lower my spirits. These include dairy products like ice cream, and chocolate-based foods. If I consume any of these at dinner, I will wake up the next morning with a malaise that can last much of the day.

What is so striking—and self-destructive—is that even while I'm eating such foods, I am aware that they'll disagree with me. Sometimes I try to convince myself that just this once I'll escape the nasty aftereffects. But deep down I know that I'm engaging in deliberate and destructive behavior. Diane is convinced that I'm allergic to chocolate in particular, and that it darkens my mood and thus harms our relationship.

My efforts to pacify my stomach can also prove troubling. My diet is quite limited, consisting mostly of fresh vegetables and fruits, fish, and occasionally chicken. As a result, I don't eat a number of foods that Diane is fond of, particularly meats such as steak or lamb chops. This is a source of disappointment and, at times, annoyance for Diane, because she misses the conviviality of a shared dish. Moreover, I think that she harbors the suspicion—echoing perhaps my father's—that I am excessively indulgent of my stomach.

As for Diane, her gastric downfall lies in what she aptly calls "junk food," like the deep-fried chicken available at carryout shops. The sudden craving for such food will descend on her at least twice a year and she'll yield to temptation in full knowledge of its ill effects. Although it may have been hypocritical of me, I used to try to reason with her using a syllogism like the following:

> Junk foods upset your stomach.
> Deep-fried chicken is a junk food.
> Ergo, deep-fried chicken will upset your stomach.

Given such indisputable logic, I suggested that Diane had no rational choice but to forgo the deep-fried chicken. Of course, she made the irrational choice. So much for syllogisms.

Even alcohol has created difficulties between us, given our respective sensitivities. It has been some years since Diane and I had a vodka or Scotch before dinner. Nowadays she will have a glass of champagne before dinner, and another with dinner, while I will have just a small glass of white wine with dinner. I know that many couples sit down together to enjoy a glass of wine before dinner, and regret that my limited consumption of alcohol may dampen the festive atmosphere that goes along with the anticipation of dinner together.

# Diane

You would think that talking or writing about food would be one of the easier exercises, because eating is one of the world's great pleasures. But when the subject of food is combined with the subject of marriage, the conversation changes radically.

When John and I first began to date, we shared an appreciation for good food—and drink, I might add. At first we went to many restaurants, enjoying everything, including fresh fish, good steak, a delicate quenelle, or a savory pizza. We experimented with new restaurants, tasting and sharing, talking and drinking. John was far more adventurous than I, since he'd been exposed to a greater range of foods.

Shortly after we met, his aunt loaned him her home in Georgetown, complete with a full kitchen. That's when we began to cook together.

John was quite comfortable in the kitchen, in part, I believe, because his father enjoyed cooking and creating new dishes. My own efforts in preparing meals for myself consisted of little more than spooning out cottage cheese with canned fruit and boiling or scrambling eggs.

John introduced me to foods I'd never tasted, such as artichokes, oysters, clams, pomegranates, and veal kidneys. We delighted in trying new recipes together, and eagerly awaited Craig Claiborne's Sunday *New York Times Magazine* food column. We broiled, braised, stewed, and fried. And all the while John was right there beside me, chopping, paring, and slicing, enjoying the aromas and anticipating a good meal. I was happy to cook and to taste anything and everything. Ultimately, I became a fairly accomplished cook, making breads, pies, cakes, as well as a variety of sophisticated dishes. We had many dinner parties during those early years, and guests were always quite complimentary.

A few years into our marriage, John began complaining of stomach problems, saying he believed that certain foods didn't agree with him. When his problems first began (in law school, he tells me), he tried some medications, but they apparently did little to ease the discomfort. Actually, both of us had various stomach problems that came and went, but I paid less attention to my own, even though I knew I should. I loved the taste of food too much to sacrifice the pleasure in order to avoid the pain. But John felt differently. As a result, little by little he began to cut down on the kinds of foods he would eat. Alcohol consumption was eliminated almost entirely, as well as what I consider the "fun" foods like fried chicken and pizza. No longer was there a willingness to experiment with new recipes. Rather, he came to rely on a narrow stable of favorites, foods he felt were less irritating to his system.

At first, when John began to develop his new approach to food, I found myself both sad and resentful. In my sensitivity, it seemed as though eliminating the shared foods was one more way for John to express his separateness, his lack of interest in being totally "in" the marriage. I had seen food as one of the basic elements of life that we could share. Now I saw food as symbolic of many of the problems we were experiencing. I felt that the food I prepared and offered was being rejected, and it felt like a rejection of me. I also found myself somewhat embarrassed, when we were invited out for dinner, by his abstemious manner of eating, and his refusal, most of the time, to accept even a small glass of wine. When we went to dinner at the home of good friends, he would sometimes take his own dinner along and eat a meal totally different from what everyone else was being served. For a long time, that got to me.

These days, while we continue to prepare the evening meal together, it's apt to consist of two entirely different offerings, one for him, which he prepares, and one for me, which I prepare. In other words, though we do sit down at the dinner table together, we tend to eat quite different foods. So food, one of the joys we shared early on, has become less of a shared experience and more a question of what pleases each of us individually.

Slowly, perhaps as individual experiences with food allergies have become more widely understood, I realize that John is not alone in his keen attention to diet. Increasingly, others have voiced the same kinds of problems, and may even go so far as to alert a hostess that there is a particular difficulty. Though I'm saddened by the thought that we can't enjoy the range and variety of foods that we once did, I've come to accept the fact that this is John's problem and he is taking care of it in the best way he knows how. And his careful attention to diet has made me more aware of, and more conscientious about, my own. My own stomach problems have been around for years and years, but I haven't cared to pay the kind of attention to them that John has. Now, thanks to John, that has changed, and I too am becoming a less foolhardy consumer of food.

# Dialogue on Food

JOHN: Somewhat surprisingly, I still find the activity of preparing food and dining with members of the family to be very important. But memories of one's own childhood—you and I have had debates about whose rice pudding is better, my mother's or yours—bring an emotional undercurrent to the act of preparing and eating food.

DIANE: You and I never anticipated that there was going to be that kind of distress, if I can put it that way, with food. When we first began to date, we had such *fun* cooking. You introduced me to so many things, and you liked to cook. And I loved to be in the kitchen. As time went on and I began to learn to cook, some of the foods agreed with you and some didn't.

JOHN: Yes, I did change, though I'm not clear why. You've thought it had to do with my father's death. When it came to food, I shifted from my paternal model to my maternal model. My father was quite a creative amateur chef, my mother constantly preoccupied with a delicate stomach, serving healthy, simple meals, with few sauces. At some point, perhaps after my father's death, I began to emulate my mother's mores. That began to change the way you and I ate.

DIANE: The issue of just having a drink before dinner! You and I used to have martinis, as I recall—

JOHN: —or, in my case, Scotch and water—

DIANE: —and it used to be such a relaxing moment for both of us. The day would ease away. Remember, for Christmases we used to take all kinds of wines up to the farm for your father to sample. My point being that up until the time he died, we used to enjoy a drink together, or a glass of wine. Then you gave up the wine and turned to mineral water. I think that began your pattern of changing your foods, eating more lightly, your mother's mode rather than your father's. Whereas my foods, healthy or unhealthy as they may be, are more wide-ranging than yours.

JOHN: I want to come at this from a different angle, namely, that meals became a time to pursue parental and familial issues. I can remember that my mother and father would choose mealtime to air some of their problems and grievances. I would sit there, largely silent, having to endure what could be at times sharp disagreements while I was trying to eat. So for me, eating has always been somewhat problematical. In our family, Diane, we made a decision, which was to use breakfast—when we could all get together—to discuss controversial issues. That made for some fairly tense breakfasts, and my stomach wasn't happy about that. So there's a degree of concern that I bring to the table and the otherwise lovely ritual of dining. I've often wondered whether that's true of others, namely, using meals as a battleground.

DIANE: By contrast, for you and me the time of food preparation has been a time when we've experienced some of our closest moments. I can think of standing there in the kitchen with you, week after week, chopping vegetables for soup. We've had the same kind of fun working together outdoors in our beautiful garden.

JOHN: I agree, and I'd even use the word "therapeutic." I've always felt that these simple actions are particularly satisfying, because you can take carrots, turnips, and celery, and turn them into a simple but delicious meal. So the preparation is just as important as the consumption. Or you can plant a rosebush and watch it grow over the years.

DIANE: You and I have reached a point where we basically eat separate foods. We sit down together every night that we don't go out, but we're eating separate foods. You've chosen yours and I've chosen mine. But increasingly I find myself moving toward *your* way of eating.

JOHN: Now that has really surprised me. For years you were the one who wanted the rich roasts, the steaks, the lamb chops, and I, for a number of reasons, became less interested in meat and more drawn to fish and vegetables. But somewhat to my surprise, you've come around to my diet, and I have to confess, in a paradoxical way, it makes me a little sad. Not that I would've gone back to eating those rich dishes, but I hated to see you give up things like that marvelous veal kidney stew my father used to make. So we gain and we lose, but we move forward.

DIANE: But forty-two years together means that food has become an important and integral part of the marital structure.

JOHN: I think food is equivocal in that respect. It can help strengthen the marital relationship, but it can also work to weaken it. I think at times when you and I have been at odds over the issue of food and diet, it's been weakened. In recent years, it's been strengthened.

DIANE: Why do you think you and I were at odds over food?

JOHN: I don't have a clear answer, but I would guess that, unconsciously, food was another occasion or pretext for manifesting, if not resolving, our differences. It did become, to a certain extent, a battleground between us.

DIANE: Do you think that most couples think about food in those terms?

JOHN: Well, that's my thesis, that most people don't *think* about it, but in fact are caught up in strong feelings, going way back into the past and continuing into the present. And their difficulties and grievances find their way into the cuisine.

DIANE: I don't think most people regard food as part of the whole mix of the relationship, yet it's such an integral part.

JOHN: Of the many illusions that each of us carries about our relationships, one is that eating is a time of pleasure and relative neutrality, and that people sit down peaceably. But the point I'm making is that inevitably, as you just suggested, these difficulties and problems do affect the ritualistic experience of eating three times a day.

DIANE: So I brought to my relationship with you a childhood memory of sitting down and eating pretty much alone. I don't remember, except for special holidays, sitting down and having a meal with my entire family. Perhaps that's why I made such a point of wanting to have all of us together for meals. At first it was only breakfast, but later on it was dinner as well, because you could be at home. Dinners then became a time for airing grievances and tensions.

JOHN: There've been times when you or I have abruptly left the dining table—although not so often when the kids were present. For a couple there are few overt gestures as alienating as getting up from the table and saying, "I don't want to eat with you. I'm going upstairs or into the library to eat by myself." That's a heavy blow.

DIANE: You're right about that. I can remember doing it, and I remember your doing it. That moment of alienation is sharply defined. You're taking away a moment when you assume there will be togetherness and sharing.

JOHN: That's our desire. That's our expectation. But it doesn't come about easily, and I think every family needs to learn its own rules and disciplines to encourage meals as a happy communal affair.

# In-Laws

## John

In marrying Diane, I was spared the need to cope—for better or for worse—with a mother- or father-in-law. Diane's mother and father had both died before I knew her. Moreover, I had little to do with her relatives, numerous as they were. Diane saw her older sister infrequently, usually at Christmastime with her family. By the time we met, Diane had also broken away from her Christian-Arab community in Washington, D.C. On rare occasions, like a wedding or a funeral, I would be thrown into a sea of aunts and uncles. In effect, Diane brought no relatives to our marriage, with the exception of her cousin by marriage, Vicky Aed, who has remained a good friend.

My father and mother were both alive when Diane and I were married. My father lived for six years, and my mother for thirty years, after our marriage. They had a significant—but not always benign—influence upon our relationship. Otherwise I presented Diane with no siblings or other relatives who played any substantial role in our lives. Thus our extended family consisted only of my father and mother.

In retrospect, I can see that the manner in which we spent our honeymoon anticipated the pleasures and pains that lay ahead. Since our wedding took place in Washington on the nineteenth of December, I suggested—perhaps unwisely—that we go to my parents' farm in Pennsylvania to celebrate both our wedding and Christmas. The setting was idyllic, with deep snow blanketing the countryside, a wood fire blazing in the fireplace, and fine food and wine on the table.

My father and Diane took to each other immediately. My mother had attended our wedding in Washington, but not my father—he couldn't get away from the chore of milking his small herd of cows twice a day. Diane was therefore particularly anxious to meet him. When we got to the farm through heavy snow, my father was attending to the cows in the barn.

When Diane entered the barn, my father instantly gave her a warm enveloping hug. That one loving and unquestioning gesture epitomized their relationship. My father found her spirited, intelligent, and attractive. He was particularly tickled by the fact that she was of Arab descent, since he had acquired a fondness for Arabs during his participation in the North African campaign in World War II. Until his death, the two of them had an easy and affectionate relationship, sharing a common interest in current events, gourmet cooking, and literature. I've often thought how much pleasure he, himself a journalist, would have taken in Diane's professional success.

My mother's relationship with Diane was, unhappily, different from my father's, contributing to some of the serious tensions in our marriage. From my perspective, my mother was admiring but jealous of Diane, sympathetic yet distant. As a feminist who had participated in suffragists' demonstrations, my mother was genuinely proud of Diane's various talents and accomplishments. And like Diane, she had never obtained a college degree, and was largely self-taught. Like Diane, she had fled her family's repressive Victorian culture. My mother could therefore appreciate the intense efforts that underlay Diane's success.

Yet my mother was in certain ways hostile to Diane. Although I didn't want to admit it, my mother resented the fact that Diane had replaced her in my life. During my adolescence in World War II, I grew up with only my mother, since my father was serving abroad in the Office of War Information. Although I was not a "mama's boy," I was certainly close to her during those formative years. I was the center of her life, and she never came to terms with my marriage to Diane.

Moreover, at some level I think my mother found it difficult to accept Diane's career. She herself had entertained ideas of doing some writing, but little came of them. With comparably few advantages, Diane had been able to establish herself professionally. This, combined with her beauty, flair for clothes, and good health, made Diane seem a formidable daughter-in-law. Thus the relationship between the two was a troubled one, with each woman probably underestimating the other's sensitivities and vulnerabilities.

I reacted to the tensions between them as I had to those between my mother and father. In each case, I was a little boy confronting two looming, unruly adults. In particular, I was caught in a cross fire between two people I loved. I internalized my anger at both of them for their stupid behavior. Above all, I experienced a sense of helplessness: I was desperate to stop the conflict yet powerless to do so. As a result, I adopted an essentially passive strategy. I would hope that the clashes would subside and, when they did flare up, I sought neutral ground, thereby helping none of the three players.

# Diane

I look back on my relationship with my mother- and father-in-law with very mixed feelings. First of all, I didn't have an opportunity to meet either of them before John and I decided to marry. My mother-in-law came to Washington from her home in Brooklyn only the night before the wedding. Because "Pop" was milking a dozen cows, he wasn't able to attend.

John was living in Georgetown at the time of our marriage, and I shall never forget the evening I first met his mother. It was a cold, wet night, and as I sat in the foyer of the house on R Street, taking off my boots, Mary Rehm came slowly down the long flight of stairs. I heard her voice before I saw her, and I'll never forget her words, because they struck me as somewhat odd in both tone and content. "Oh," she said, "Scoop didn't tell me you were so pretty."

She didn't say "Hello," or "How nice to meet you," or anything of the sort. Perhaps I should have been flattered by her words, but I sensed that they weren't intended to be friendly or welcoming. I immediately stood to meet her gaze and reach out my hand to her. Her own was thin and delicate. Her eyes were a faded blue and her hair bright red—the stunning characteristics of a tall woman of sixty-one who looked at least twenty years younger. She carried herself beautifully, and it was easy to imagine her walking down a runway in 1920s Paris, where I knew she had been a fashion model. As she kept up a light non-stop chatter, a practice I realized was the product of her own nervousness, we moved into the living room where the two of us sat down while Scoop (she never called him anything else) lit a fire.

As we sat together, I could feel her gaze, knowing she was scrutinizing me, wondering what kind of wife I would be for her son. That sense of "being appraised" stayed with me throughout that evening, the wedding day, and later, when we went to be with her and Pop at the farm for our honeymoon. Why I agreed to such an arrangement I'll never understand, except that I'd heard so much about the beauty of the farm and longed to see the place that meant so much to John.

Meeting Pop was a totally different experience. When we reached the farmhouse, it was around five-thirty in the afternoon, and Pop was out in the barn milking the cows. After we'd gone into the house and seen the beauty of the fire and the lovely Christmas greens adorning the living room, John and I walked to the barn, and there was Pop, arms wide open, welcoming and warm. From that moment on, he called me *"ma belle fille,"* and we loved each other.

I have fond memories of those first days at the farm, despite the fact that I felt Mary was continuing to watch me, using every opportunity to ask about my background, my family, and my education. At one point I was taken aback when she said, "Well now, Diane dear, you're very charming and beautiful, but what are you *really* like?" Before I could think of what to say, John stepped in and said, somewhat critically, "Mom! What kind of a question is that? What you see is who and what Diane is." Pop jumped in as well, and I felt relieved that I hadn't had to respond to her.

In the first few years of our marriage, Mary became a friend and supporter. We wrote to each other frequently concerning mundane matters, including the fact that John was working so much while I was at home with first David and then Jennie. She came to visit occasionally and stayed for several weeks at a time and we would sit together mending old sheets or turning the collars on John's shirts to extend their wear. We were easy with each other as we talked about generalities, but at the same time we were wary.

There were many occasions when I felt she stayed with us for too long a time, but I wouldn't have dreamed of asking her to shorten her stays until much later in our marriage. It wasn't a long trip for her: she was traveling from New York, a four-hour train ride at most. But she fretted so before each visit that it finally made more sense for John to go up to New York to get her and bring her down by air. In our first home, there were just two bedrooms, but we managed to create a comfortable room for her in the lower part of the house, which she found quite cozy and private.

Later, when Jennie and David were a bit older, difficulties began to emerge. First, Mary made it clear that her affection for David was greater than what she felt for Jennie. Perhaps that happens in many families, but she made no secret of her preference, and would say things in Jennie's presence that were terribly wounding. Second, when she was around, John behaved differently. He was cooler, less affectionate, and plain uptight when Mary was in the house. I've talked with other wives whose husbands experienced a similar sense of unease when their mothers were around. Mary would focus her entire attention on him, recalling experiences the two of them had had together as John was growing up, while Pop was away at war. John, for his part, would do nothing to turn the conversation away from himself or her. It became increasingly frustrating.

When Pop died in 1967, I was heartbroken, feeling as if I'd lost someone unique in my life. He had loved and cared about me, and had been someone I could talk to and laugh with easily. After he died, Mary seemed to rely increasingly on John, and he, of course, felt that as an only child, he had to make sure she was cared for and comfortable. She would call on the phone, never saying anything other than "Is Scoop there?" Stunned by her lack of warmth, I would simply pass the phone to John.

Finally, when she was in her upper seventies and not in the best of health, we urged her to move to Washington, to an apartment complex owned and operated by the Episcopal church, not far from our home. It took several years of persuasion, and finally, after several hospitalizations requiring us to go back and forth to New York, she reluctantly agreed to move. I believe the move saved—and extended—her life. After several months of difficult adjustment on her part, she began to get into the rhythm of Washington's cultural life, visiting art galleries and attending concerts, moving easily by bus or subway to the downtown area. I'm glad we were able to facilitate the move for her, and to make the last years of her life more comfortable, but I also believe that her proximity and presence in our lives for those years between 1977 and 1990 made our already tension-filled marriage even more difficult.

# Dialogue on In-Laws

DIANE: If there is one area in which I have a great sadness, combined with anger, it was the way you did nothing about your mother and her treatment of me. As you say clearly in your essay, you felt you were *caught* and couldn't do anything to allay the problem. So you did nothing. Whereas I, as your wife, expected, and believed very strongly, that your responsibility was to your wife and to your family. The fact that you didn't speak up to your mother about her treatment of me and about her treatment of Jennie makes me very sad to think about even today.

JOHN: Well, that's quite a strong statement. In my defense, I felt that we were dealing with an elderly, somewhat frail woman, who'd had a number of difficulties in her own life. I thought you had the greater strength and stamina. I recall so vividly my sense of being torn between the two of you and the feeling that she didn't have that many years left, and that if I had to indulge one or the other, I would indulge my mother.

DIANE: From the beginning, she gave you—as well as Pop and me—indications that she was going to make it difficult for me, and she did. I cannot agree with your statement that she wasn't well, because she was a strong woman who had suffered from headaches. She lived until she was ninety-two. I have to tell you, the happiness we lost together because of her leaves me very resentful, even of her memory.

JOHN: When she was present, there certainly were problems, but you're suggesting that these extended into our relationship when she wasn't even around?

DIANE: Oh my gosh, when she called on the telephone and I would pick it up, she would say, "Is Scoop there?" She wouldn't ask how I was, or how the children were. She just wanted to speak with you. As far as your mother was concerned, there was a narrowness of vision on your part, and she took advantage of it right from the start.

JOHN: What can I say?

DIANE: Perhaps you might say something to help other people who are struggling with the same kind of difficulty. It was very hard, as though you ignored the passage in the Book of Genesis that says, "Therefore a man leaves his father and his mother and cleaves to his wife, and they become one flesh." It was as though you felt you could not break from her.

JOHN: What you're saying is that you would have had me raise the issue with her and try to—what? Work out a more tolerable relationship?

DIANE: I think what you might have done was to make a simple statement: "Mom, Diane is my wife. I love her. I love our family. And I wish you, Mom, would be more thoughtful about how you treat her and our family."

JOHN: We can't change the past, it's done. I'm tempted to say at this point that, yes, I should have raised these issues with her, which I didn't do, or didn't do to the extent you would have had me do.

DIANE: I know how hard this is for you. I know you loved your mother very much and she adored you. If you had it to do over again, considering what you know now, at age seventy-one, what do you think you might do differently?

JOHN: I would probably raise, in some fashion, the issues you've identified, particularly her relationship with you and her relationship with Jennie. While she was still in Brooklyn, we didn't see her that often. She would make occasional trips, but I guess I felt that the difficulties, such as they were, could be restricted to brief periods throughout the year, and therefore didn't have to influence our relationship in any appreciable way. Once she came to Washington, she would be in our home fairly infrequently. I made a practice, as you know, of seeing her alone every Sunday. There again I felt that I could avoid any oppressive influence she might have had on the family and on our relationship. Maybe that was unrealistic, but that was the effort I made, that I would be with her for an hour or two each Sunday, and otherwise we would relate to ourselves in the normal way.

DIANE: When I would raise these issues with you, you dismissed me. It really upset me, and you thought I was being silly! And you said, "Well, she's just an old woman and she wants to—"

JOHN: Yes, I thought then, and I think now, we could indulge her.

DIANE: It was an "indulgence" that offended your wife. The point I'm making is that you were not willing to take up any of my concerns with her.

JOHN: I guess it was a fundamental difference of perspective. These actions on her part that you felt so strongly about at the time, and to some degree still do, I didn't see as serious issues. They didn't seem to me to go to the heart of our relationship, as you feel they did. I guess I had two hypersensitive women on my hands.

DIANE: One was your wife.

JOHN: And I was trying to do justice to both of them, in some evenhanded way. You saw that as an unfair and hurtful indulgence at your expense. I guess I thought that you didn't have to dwell on these issues as much as you did then, and clearly still do now. It was a matter of accommodation, and I didn't accommodate you sufficiently. Yes, if she were alive today, I think, on the strength of greater reflection and experience, I could raise some of these issues. I can't disagree with you that that would have been not only the appropriate but the most efficacious way to proceed. Two of my most serious problems were that I felt torn, without knowing quite where to go, between career and family and, most certainly, between you and Mom. I felt stretched and tried, perhaps unrealistically, to create two domains: one was yours, and the other was hers.

DIANE: She didn't want to see me in that last year of her life. When she was beginning to decline, I went with you to see her on a couple of Sundays. She finally said to you that she just wanted to see you. And you let that go, and you went to see her by yourself. You couldn't tell your mother that her behavior toward me was unacceptable.

JOHN: It would have been difficult for me to do so. I wish I had pursued some of these issues with her, particularly because I know they've hurt you so. Do you think it would have helped me deal with my mother if your mother had remained alive?

DIANE: That's a great question. Perhaps it would've. Maybe if I hadn't been left with such sadness about my own mother's death, and the difficult relationship she and I had had throughout my life, maybe I wouldn't have been so hurt by your mother's rejection of me. It was as though it happened to me twice in my life, and when it came from your mother the second time, it was more than I could take. It also caused a major rift between us, which seemed to be yet a third rejection. I'm glad we've written and talked about this. It's time for me to let go of the anger.

JOHN: You see, I approached my mother as though I were her only friend, and while she did have friends, she relied on me more than anybody else. I guess that's another reason why I felt I couldn't raise these painful issues, because she relied on me so. I was the dutiful son, and maybe excessively dutiful. Perhaps lurking here, in Freudian terms, is an incomplete separation from the mother figure. That probably plays a role here. My effort was to keep in separate worlds two women who had this difficult relationship.

DIANE: Do you believe that since your mother died, you and I have had a closer relationship?

JOHN: I think we have become closer in recent years. Whether there's a causal relationship between her death and our drawing closer, I'm not sure.

DIANE: My guess is that her death finally freed you in some ways to be a fully loving husband, because you no longer felt torn.

JOHN: There's some sense to that. I agree that my preoccupation certainly disappeared. My concern was seeing that she was taken care of and could still lead a reasonably rewarding life. At the same time, I am genuinely sorry that in pursuing that concern, I hurt you so.

# Sleep

## John

Marital sleep. The very words conjure up in my mind an image of special intimacy. Diane and I are sharing a large and comfortable bed covered by a canopy that creates a snug refuge. With a few words or gestures and a final kiss, I share my descent into sleep with Diane. She, in turn, does the same, and the two of us together yield to sweet fatigue. In fact, until about ten years ago, this was just how we shared our sleep.

How harsh the present reality seems by contrast. I fall asleep quickly, but my sleep is apt to be restless and punctuated by snoring. Diane increasingly finds sleep elusive, and must therefore create a calm and quiet environment. As a result, practical considerations prevail over the romantic, and most of the time Diane and I now sleep apart in separate beds.

This vignette is charged with a number of more than superficial feelings on my part. When we try to share the same bed, past failures to fall asleep together leave me anxious. At a time when I should be gradually losing consciousness, I find myself excessively alert. Diane will be sensitive to even a slight shift in my position. This concern prompts an internal debate over whether I should risk the shift. Which should prevail, Diane's repose or my comfort? In short, I'm working to ensure that both of us fall asleep, knowing that this effort will only retard the process. I then feel guilty that I'm depriving Diane not only of sleep but of a shared pleasure. Through no fault of hers, I've unwittingly set out to assure her a good night's rest, yet I'm unable to bring that about.

In this process, I become aware of a feeling of sadness mixed with irritation. I genuinely regret that we can't achieve the romantic image; I know how strongly Diane is drawn to it, as am I. At the same time, her hypersensitivity to motion and sound grates on me. If she weren't such a light sleeper, I tell myself, we would be able to share the bed more often. I have now justified the conclusion that our failure to do so is her fault.

If truth be known, I am ambivalent about sharing a bed with Diane for sleeping. I too am attracted to the romantic image. As I did during my boyhood, though, I do enjoy falling asleep alone, undisturbed by any concern for someone else's comfort and rest. I'm somewhat uncomfortable about this selfish pleasure, particularly when Diane periodically talks about purchasing new twin beds.

# Diane

There are few things in this world more deliciously satisfying than a good night's sleep. As I anticipate those hours of peace and rest, I'm immediately calmed, knowing that I will get under soft sheets and comforter, read for a few moments, turn off the light, and drift into ultimate relaxation.

Those feelings represent for me a dramatic change that has taken place in the past few years. For decades I wrestled with insomnia, dreading even the thought of getting into bed, knowing that I would fall asleep quickly and awaken a few hours later. Then, frustrated, I would turn on the light, read, try to go back to sleep, turn off the light, and start the whole process over again. Meanwhile John lay next to me, dreaming the dreams of the peaceful and snoring slightly. I would get up in the morning feeling and looking tired, irritable, and unwell. It took me decades to come to the realization that I simply couldn't sleep well lying in the same bed with John, a thorny issue for me and for him.

As newlyweds, we had no problem sharing a double (*not* queen- or king-size) bed. Later we purchased a queen-size bed, and for a time all was well. But as the children and we grew older, my sleeping life became increasingly problematic. Every single movement John made in the bed wakened me. Moreover, each time one of the children got up to use the bathroom, or coughed, or sneezed, my eyes would pop open. It was hard on the children because they worried about waking me up. Once awakened, I couldn't fall back to sleep. It became intolerable.

Finally I made the decision to move into an adjoining, quieter room. While I was close by (and "visiting privileges" were understood), I felt guilty. I felt embarrassed. Deep down, I felt I'd somehow abandoned a sacred place in our marital relationship. When friends talked about sleeping in their beds together, I pretended to myself that John and I were together in our bed. I said nothing to make it clear that we were no longer sharing the same bed. It felt like a failure. Why *couldn't* I manage to overcome this problem? Why was I such a *light* sleeper?

Well, I wish I knew the answer to that question. What I do know is that many women—and some men—share this problem. I have read first-person articles about the difficulty of sleeping in the same bed with another person. It works for some. It clearly doesn't work for me. In any event, both John and I are now resting comfortably—he, because he no longer has to worry about my sleep or feel guilty about his slight snoring, and I, because I can look forward to a peaceful and restful sleep each and every night.

# Dialogue on Sleep

JOHN: As I think about marital sleep, I'm reminded of that old expression: if it weren't so serious, it would be funny. Well, the fact is, marital sleep is both. There are innumerable jokes about couples sleeping together or apart. And many magazine ads and television programs portray happy couples sleeping together. But the thing that puzzles me is why we place this enormous importance on sleeping in the same bed when it's a matter of sharing only a few minutes as we drift off, and perhaps a few more minutes as we awaken. Otherwise we're unconscious and oblivious to each other.

DIANE: Well, *would* that we were unconscious and oblivious to each other. We reached a point in our marriage when I could no longer be unconscious and oblivious. So, given that fact and granted that I am clearly a light sleeper, it made sense for the two of us to sleep in separate beds and to enjoy the healing process of sleep. I just felt so guilty moving out of the bedroom after so many years, as though I had deserted the marital bed and were somehow traitorous. And yet we enjoy those moments in the morning, or before we go to sleep at night, lying in the same bed together, talking and chortling and playing together. But during the night, sleep is sleep, and it's a necessity.

JOHN: Yes, but you've just used the word "guilt." Where does this enormous importance that we attach to sleeping together come from? Is it the bed and mattress manufacturers?

DIANE: [*laughter*] It's all those sexy movies and television programs!

JOHN: Well, it's certainly part of our culture. But I'm raising a rather serious question, because I think you and I are probably fairly typical, wrestling with the practical need for sleep and, at the same time, pursuing this illusion of the bliss of sleeping together. It does seem as though there's an inordinate importance attached to it.

DIANE: Let's face it: there are lots of people who are heavy sleepers and can enjoy being wrapped around each other during the night. You and I just happen not to be that kind of couple. But for those who can do it, I think it *is* blissful. I think it's wonderful. A friend told me the other day, because her husband is now at home each morning instead of running off to the office, that he said to her when she got up, "Oh, do you really have to get up? Let's *snuggle* a little more." Well, you and I snuggle in the mornings, but we cannot snuggle at night and sleep. That's all there is to it.

JOHN: I think the strength of the illusion of happy, conjoined sleep is part of the problem here. Obviously sleep is vital, and we need it badly. And yet some couples keep chasing this illusion to their harm, because they feel guilty or sad when the illusion isn't realized.

DIANE: When the kids were really young, we'd be so tired from getting up in the middle of the night and feeding them that we'd fall back into our small double bed, totally exhausted, and go right back to sleep. As we got older, I began to sleep far less heavily. Perhaps it was a matter of habit, listening so carefully for the children's noises at night. But I think you're right, that there's some kind of illusion out there that a happy relationship entails sleeping together in the same bed. If two people happen to move into separate beds or separate rooms, it's as though there's something wrong with them and that they don't share the kind of intimacy that others do.

JOHN: In our case, the combination of my snoring and restless limbs literally drove you from the bedroom. The fact that we do, for the most part, sleep apart, and then come together on mornings when we have more leisure time, for me that rather enhances those times. If I could lay down a new expectation—

DIANE: Oh dear . . .

JOHN and DIANE: [*laughter*]

JOHN: —I would urge people in a serious relationship to understand that there is perhaps—I offer this as a hypothesis—some kind of natural evolution. In the early years of a marriage, for a variety of reasons, physical and otherwise, people can sleep together. And then, later, they may move into separate beds or separate rooms. But we don't have to sit around wringing our hands because we think we don't have an ideal sleeping existence. In short, I'm telling people as they grow older in their relationships, take it easy, and don't lay such a trip on yourself.

DIANE: Well, I think I did lay a trip on myself. But once we created this different kind of arrangement for ourselves, we both came to accept the fact that I felt better, and you felt better *because* I felt better. We could then more laughingly and enjoyably come together when we did, instead of waking each morning in frustration because I hadn't been able to sleep.

JOHN: Yes, I think another way of putting this is that we were finally able to put happy sleep in the context of the larger relationship. To go on trying to stay together in sleep wouldn't have made much sense. We finally realized it was the larger relationship that counted. And that for the sake of that relationship, we had to make a variety of adjustments. I think this may have been one of the more natural adjustments, one which didn't impair, and, in fact, enhanced, the relationship.

DIANE: But, you know, when we're on vacations, and in twin beds, we manage quite well. So that leads me to wonder whether, at some point, we might come back to sharing the same room, but in separate beds.

JOHN: Well, that *would* be lovely.

# The Third Person

## John

Our marriage, like most—I'm tempted to say all—has been vulnerable to attack by both internal and external forces. Internal forces include alienation, dissension, and insensitivity. Among external forces are physical ailments, excessive work demands, and divisive behavior on the part of relatives. Such forces can try a marriage sorely, and even put the couple's love to the test.

Perhaps the most corrosive, in my experience, is the strong attraction that may arise between one of the partners and a third person. In most cases, the degree of attraction will be moderate and tolerable—that is, it will enliven one spouse's relationship with the third person without jeopardizing the spouses' fidelity to each other. In particular, the spouse may feel free to flirt with the third person within bounds acceptable to both spouses.

But what if, as I have experienced, the attraction is both strong and reciprocal? That is, if the third person and I find ourselves drawn to each other to an unexpectedly strong degree? At the same time, we profess no intention of disrupting existing relationships. However naive we may be, we do so in good faith, committed to refraining from overt infidelity. In this situation, I've found myself confronting some fundamental and difficult questions.

The most immediate and perhaps most challenging question is whether—and to what extent—I should tell Diane about my relationship with the third person. In the abstract, the answer seems simple. If our relationship is to be honest and vital, it demands openness, particularly when it may be challenged by an outside force. Diane and I can't preserve our relationship if one withholds pertinent information from the other. Anything less than candor can only weaken the bonds between us.

In fact, however, the abstract answer proves all the more glib because it doesn't take into account my fragility and perhaps Diane's as well. I approach the question weighed down by both guilt and fear. My guilt springs from a troubling sense of inadequacy. If I were wholly and truly faithful to Diane, I wouldn't be so drawn to the third person in the first place. It must be some deficiency in me that makes me vulnerable.

I'm also afraid that my disclosure to Diane will provoke harsh words and bitter feelings on her part. Diane sets great store by loyalty, and she will regard my dalliance as an act of blatant infidelity. Nor will I be able to plead innocent, since the effect of my actions—viewed in even the most sympathetic light—is undeniably subversive. Thus, without defense, I will fearfully bear and deserve her condemnation.

Whether I should tell Diane also bears on her sensitivity. That is, if my relationship with the third person seems under control, why not spare Diane the pain of disclosure? Maintaining her ignorance, however, may prove difficult. She will almost certainly have the opportunity to observe the interaction between the third person and me. If, as is likely, she senses the attraction, then the failure to disclose it will only add insult to injury.

Wrestling with my conflicting feelings, I settled on a ragged compromise. On the one hand, I did disclose or, rather, acknowledge the relationship to Diane, since she already had inklings of it. On the other hand, I didn't try to explore with her the reasons for the attraction and what I—and we—might learn from it. In retrospect, I think it would have caused less harm to our marriage if I had been able to share the experience with Diane, instead of confronting her with it.

The unavoidable question, of course, is why I was so drawn to the third person. Although I have given this question considerable thought, I have no firm answer. I can, however, see certain aspects of the genesis of the attraction. First, it was truly irrational in the psychiatric sense of the word—that is, it had no perceptible connection whatsoever with my current state of mind. Second, the attraction was puerile, in that it seemed to relate to an early stage in my life. The third person somehow stirred childhood memories, remote and indistinct. Third, the attraction involved my mother. It was as if the third person was promising to provide some precious and missing part of my childhood. I don't know what part. I do know, however, that as a middle-aged man, I suddenly became my mother's child again, with the opportunity to renew that experience, free from all adult preoccupations and responsibilities. With the third person, I could imagine myself as playfully boyish and newly flirtatious in the company of an attractive younger woman.

In time, the attraction ebbed and died, primarily as a result of Diane's pain and my shame. Did the experience strengthen our marriage? I am not sure that survival is a form of strengthening. I do believe, however, that sooner or later, most spouses must deal, as best they can, with the presence and potential threat of a third person. If possible, it is better for both to do so together than one alone.

# Diane

Secrets. They can kill a relationship. They undermine that fragile fabric that two people attempt to create together. Secrets begin as tiny points in the mind, but slowly they expand, taking up more and more space, time, thought, and energy.

I have postponed writing this essay as long as possible. It's so hard to acknowledge both the pain and the shame that the subject brings to my heart and mind. Pain, because I felt betrayed by John's strong feelings of attraction to another woman. Shame, because I betrayed my husband by my strong feelings for another man. Why did it happen in my own case? Why did it happen in his?

Perhaps there's no rational way to explain such feelings. For myself, I believe they arose out of a need for attention, warmth, affection, and excitement that was not being satisfied in the primary relationship. John's work life seemed to draw him further and further away from me. I turned to outside volunteer activities to satisfy my desire for companionship, laughter, and friendship. But right from the beginning, I had a sense that my initially

innocent flirtation with a friend (is *any* flirtation truly innocent?) would become increasingly important to me. I couldn't
wait to see him, and sought out every opportunity to do so,
always within the safety of a group. We made frequent eye
contact, moved toward each other, and gently touched hands
when chance allowed. He became my secret, mine alone, my
moment to dream, to imagine, to create a different existence for
myself.

It was a lovely secret inside me that began to spill over and
turn into a potentially lethal poison affecting my relationship
with John. He knew something was different. He could sense
that I had turned inward, away from him and toward the other
man. And yet we never spoke of it, as if it did not exist. We
fought bitterly, never mentioning a name. Most of the time, we
did not speak at all.

I look back on this period in our lives realizing that I was
struggling to grow, to find a way to be myself. I had allowed
myself to be defined by my marriage, not because John had
insisted on it but because I thought that was the way it should
be. Then, realizing that John could not or would not satisfy all
of my emotional needs, I began to act out a kind of rebellion
against him. After all, I said to myself, for years I'd been striving
to be the perfect mate, and he wasn't being perfect *back*! Finally,
I concluded, the marriage was never going to be enough—either
for me *or* for him. Looking for myself in a relationship with
another man did not make sense either, but it gave me a sense of
myself as a separate person, not *just* a wife, not *just* a mother, and
not one to be taken for granted.

For every action, there is a reaction. I know that my behavior
caused hurt and even grief. Whether it led—directly or other-

wise—to John's own attraction to another woman, I cannot know. I do know that we are about to have a conversation on this subject that we should have had years ago.

# Dialogue on the Third Person

JOHN: We're obviously dealing with a painful issue, but with the passage of time I think I can look back on it with a certain objectivity. In doing so, two questions emerge. The most obvious, of course, is why you were drawn to a certain man and I was drawn to a certain woman. And we can certainly talk about that. But for me, the really fascinating question is why in the world we stayed together. I don't recall ever sitting down with you, Diane, and drawing up a kind of calculus—that is, the pros and cons of our staying together. As I recall, we just gritted our teeth and saw it through, without shedding any real light on the problems.

DIANE: Oh no. I recall it differently. I think at one point we were both serious about going our separate ways. It may have been that those two relationships—which we call "the third person"—were simply the culmination of the outpouring of feeling that was taking us away from each other. They were perhaps reflective of all the internal strife that was going on, and our dissatisfaction with each other.

JOHN: Do you recall any instance when with some seriousness we discussed why we were drawn to others? Or why we should remain in the marriage and endure? Do you recall that? I don't. It seems to me we both recognized the centrifugal forces but didn't try to explore them, other than whether we should separate. But I don't even recall an in-depth discussion of that issue.

DIANE: As I said in my essay, I think this is the first time we have talked about it. Don't forget, as I shall never forget, that at one point you decided to move out of the house for a week. You took a room at a hotel downtown. I can't recall the time frame, or whether it was in the midst of all this. All I know is that we were in terrible trouble as a couple.

JOHN: I so vividly recall the taxi driving up for me as I stood at the door holding a small piece of luggage. As the driver reached the end of the block, before he turned the corner, I thought to myself, Why am I doing this? I saw it in a different light, and at that point might have told him to turn around and take me back home. Nevertheless, I did go downtown and stay in a really third-rate hotel. I think it gave me some breathing space. But I want to return to this question. Why did we endure?

DIANE: Why did we endure? For the first time, I think we looked in the face of what it would mean to be separate and on our own. I think we examined what each of us gives to the other, but we did it separately. We didn't sit down and say, "Here are the pros and cons." It was an internal battle that was going on within each of us. I was angry as hell at your behavior. It seemed to me that you weren't really paying attention to *anyone* else's feelings but your own. It was as though everything was about you. It was a narcissism that I just couldn't believe, and couldn't tolerate. So I moved into my own world, and began to think in my own terms of life without you, but not thinking about your moving out of the house permanently.

JOHN: But that still doesn't answer my question—

DIANE: Well, what is *your* answer?

JOHN: I would say, first of all, that your commitment to the relationship, your loyalty, helped me—although at times I resented it. Second, sheer stubbornness. I think in each of us there was a disinclination to give the marriage up and say it had failed. Third, I would certainly have to note the children. At some level, neither of us was willing to break up the family. There was a kind of doggedness that kept us together. Now the question is, was that love? If it was love, it was love of the very *un*romantic kind. It was a love composed of loyalty and stubbornness. It didn't feel like love. But there was something that kept us going. I look back on that with a sense of marvel.

DIANE: Do you think it was love, at an elemental level?

JOHN: I think my answer would be that, yes, it was love—an aspect of love—a love that places great emphasis on commitment and loyalty, and just plain sticking it out.

DIANE: I think we have now gotten to the heart of these discussions, which is that any relationship at times involves just sticking it out, no matter how difficult those times are. And I'm *not* talking about times when physical abuse is involved; that is an entirely different situation. But I'm talking about the commitment that is part of what makes love, what creates that bond. I certainly didn't want to see us living separately.

JOHN: But if the reader of our book should ask, "Well, how do you tell if sticking it out makes sense, on balance, and if it doesn't?" I would say it becomes nonrational. Either there's a certain adhesive that remains, or it doesn't. I don't think it would have been a clearly unreasonable or irrational act, Diane, for us to separate. Goodness knows, there were reasons for doing so.

DIANE: You know, it was at a time in this country when divorce was occurring frequently, and people accepted the idea that if your marriage doesn't work, you move on to someone else. But I wasn't about to be a serial marrier. I had had one marriage that failed, I wasn't going to have a second. But *you* had to be part of that. You keep asking me why we stayed together. I do believe that deep down you have to respond to that question with your heart. It was beyond commitment. There had to be something in you that said, "This marriage is important to who I am."

JOHN: I think that's well put. The strain in me to be the loner, the fellow who goes off by himself, who endures life as it comes—that did become subordinated to the importance of the family, that is, of you and the children. I guess I *grew up* and began to identify and value aspects of life in a family which I hadn't fully appreciated before.

DIANE: That's not to say that any relationship fully and completely recovers. One can forgive, but one never forgets; it's something that always dwells somewhere in the mind. Each time a question or a doubt surfaces, I find myself having to actively put it aside. Don't think that forty-two years of marriage are enough to put those feelings aside permanently. At some level, perhaps out of my own sense of insecurity, they'll always be there. You're a *wonderful* man, an attractive man, people love you. But I will always feel in my heart the resentment that occurred over your relationship with the other woman, when I never believed there could be such a relationship.

JOHN: I also *then* resented—and time has alleviated this—your relationship with the other man. That was really a terrible blow. It just knocked the underpinnings out of any sense of male pride or sufficiency. It was rough going. My immediate response was to retaliate in some way or to go off by myself. But back to the fundamental question: maybe it's a matter of listening to the heart rather than the head. We could have composed a fairly lengthy list of good reasons why at least a trial separation was in order, but that wasn't quite there for either of us, and the heart seems to have won out.

DIANE: Did you see it happening in my case? Did you know what was happening between me and the third person?

JOHN: I take your statement at face value that your relationship was always in a social group, and in that setting I knew exactly what was going on, but of course I wondered and worried that it might be consummated, which it wasn't.

DIANE: And I worried in the same way. I know you did have several private lunches. It was the public realm that really got to me. I could see what you were doing. I knew when she was in your presence that something was different.

JOHN: Did that knowledge help or hurt?

DIANE: Hurt! It was terrible!

JOHN: Because you felt others were observing the same thing?

DIANE: Absolutely!

JOHN: And therefore you were deeply embarrassed? Humiliated?

DIANE: Exactly. Did you have that sense?

JOHN: Certainly. I was being demeaned in the presence of others who, I was pretty sure, saw what was going on. That made it very difficult.

DIANE: Which made it even more difficult for you and me to talk about it. We couldn't talk about it. We *didn't* talk about it. Perhaps if we had talked about it . . .

JOHN: It's rather easy to say we should have or might have talked about it, but that would have been very difficult, because in my case, and perhaps in yours, the conversation would have begun from a position of being deeply wounded. And the wound was sufficiently deep that, with all of our other insecurities, it was almost an unspeakable subject.

DIANE: Well, we've now spoken about it. How do we feel now?

JOHN: I would say that, now that you and I are in a good place, it isn't that painful to look back on. And I think there are some lessons—

DIANE: Such as?

JOHN: Such as the value of looking at the entirety of the relationship—the family and the children—both the good parts and the bad parts. To assess the situation in the larger context, rather than dwell upon the immediate hurt and the immediate desire to lash back.

DIANE: You undermined my feeling of trust in you. That sense of trust vanished for a long time. It was difficult, every time you walked out the door, not to be mistrustful. It has taken me years to get over it.

JOHN: As for me, for a long time you took away my sense—my pride—of being first in your life. You have restored that, as I hope I have regained your trust.

DIANE: You have. I love you, and I trust you will never hurt me in that way again.

# Aging

## John

According to the time-honored pledge, we marry for richer for poorer, but not for younger or older. Our youth-dominated culture discourages the contemplation of old age. Even when couples are well into their years of marriage, they assume that their mental and physical condition will remain constant. In short, the certainty of old age is either denied or suppressed.

I am seventy-one years old, and Diane is sixty-five. We are in good health, of both mind and body, for which we are deeply grateful. We eat sensibly, drink moderately, and exercise reasonably, favoring walks together. We can still take on, with occasional rests, the steep back roads of northeastern Pennsylvania, where our beloved farm is located. But our bodies remind us, in undramatic but telling ways, that we are no longer in our twenties, thirties, or even forties. We are forced to give increasing attention to the inexorable process of aging.

I foresee two fairly distinct periods ahead of us. In the first, we will largely retain our present degree of freedom. That is, we'll continue to be able to use our minds and bodies with few impediments. Whether we wish to read a book, take a walk, or prepare a meal, our faculties will be available. The mind may not be quite so sharp and the body not quite so agile, but each of us will be up to the normal tasks of every passing day.

In the second period, we'll lose that freedom by degrees. We'll need help getting about. We'll have to be reminded of people and events. We'll be less able to concentrate on words and ideas. In short, we'll be reverting to the needs of childhood and our reliance on others.

I have high hopes for us in each of these two periods, especially after Diane's anticipated retirement in the next few years. In the first period they would include the following:

1. Enjoy the world while it remains open and accessible to us. This would include such activities as traveling, gardening, and spending time at our farm.
2. Inquire into, and learn about, new fields, like history, science, and the arts.
3. Enrich and cultivate relationships with family members and friends.

In the second period, my hopes would include the following:

1. Help each other to accept—and not deny—our ailments and illnesses.
2. Maintain a healthy sense of humor about the often undignified frailties of old age.
3. Learn and tell each other the full medical truth, so that we can help make intelligent decisions.

Implicit in all these hopes is the recognition that old age is part of a spiritual journey. That journey will be sustained by the love and compassion that Diane and I will continue to share throughout old age.

# Diane

As I write this, on September 11, 2001, terrorism has struck the United States. The World Trade Center towers have been destroyed in New York City by suicide terrorists flying hijacked American planes, killing thousands of people. The Pentagon has been struck by another hijacked plane, destroying one portion completely, with additional casualties. And a fourth hijacked plane went down outside Pittsburgh, and there is speculation that the target was the White House, the Capitol, or Camp David. The sense of physical security this country has enjoyed up until now has been seriously impaired.

Like many Americans hearing the news today, I realize once again how fragile life can be. No matter how carefully we manage our lives, no matter how many vitamins we take or how often we exercise, no matter how well we care for ourselves and our families, the end of life may be only seconds away. As John and I went for a walk on this sunlit, breezy day here in Washington, we spoke of Thornton Wilder's novel *The Bridge of San Luis Rey,* in which people from different backgrounds, rich and poor, meet their fate as they cross a bridge that can't support them. Dwelling on the factor of chance for even a moment leads me to reflect that all of those people who died today—September 11, 2001—went to their places of business this morning expecting that they would live to see another day.

Now, cherishing each day all the more, I am strangely optimistic about the process, and even the duration, of aging. I say "strangely" because both my parents died when they were young—my mother at forty-nine, my dad at sixty-two. For a long time I was fatalistic, believing that I too would meet an early death. It was difficult for me to approach the age of fifty, and when I passed it, I felt almost *guilty* to have lived beyond the age when my mother died. That benchmark gave me the gift of freedom. No longer would I have to dwell upon that "deadline": my life was my own to live, free of the shadows her early death had cast over me.

Now I am sixty-five, having reached a point in life that even my father didn't achieve. I ask myself why. Why did they die so young, and why should I have been given the gift of health, considering their premature endings? The answers I came up with before today were sound and helped me to face the future with optimism.

First, I haven't endured the long illnesses that plagued my mother. She died of cirrhosis of the liver, not as a result of alcohol consumption but as a long-term consequence of the malaria she contracted as a teenager in Egypt, which left her liver severely impaired. She was a depressed and angry woman, which could also have had an adverse effect on her overall health. Second, I quit smoking—in my twenties. My father suffered from extreme high blood pressure. He, like his brothers, was a lifelong smoker. He had difficulty walking because of an inherited foot deformity, so exercise was out of the question. Like his brothers, he died after a heart attack. Finally, thanks to John, I have taken good care of myself, despite the spate of unusual ailments I've experienced.

So here I am, thinking about both the future and the events of this day, which have filled me and the whole country with sadness and fear. Hence my feelings are mixed. There continues to be a certain amount of excitement. Why? Because I know that sometime in the next few years, I'll come to the end of my radio career. It's been rich, wonderful, and enormously rewarding in every way. I've had the honor of speaking with many of the world's most interesting and thoughtful people. I've worked with supportive and savvy producers. I've learned so much about so many topics that I otherwise could never have fathomed. But I know the time is coming when I'll want to move on. Then what? Who knows? But I believe there are new possibilities for growth yet to come. In what context, I cannot imagine, but then again I never imagined a career in radio.

Painting watercolors is something I began doing many years ago, with great pleasure and joy. I haven't had much time for it in the last few years, so I look forward to taking it up again. Also, I've become very interested in writing, and am planning on writing a series of letters to our grandson Benjamin so that he will have a sense of who his grandparents are. John and I haven't seen a great deal of this country, though we've traveled abroad. The older I get, the more I want to enjoy this grand and glorious country of ours, in both a historic and visual sense, and to begin to appreciate its extensive beauty and variety. I hope to be able to get up in the morning and fully read the morning newspaper, and then, in my nightgown, walk through our garden at a leisurely pace, as I quite often do now on summer mornings, appreciating and tending to the shrubs, trees, and flowers that have become such an important part of my life. I want to spend more time with our children and their families, participating, but never interfering, in their lives. I have so many things I want to do.

Of course, at this age, I also think about the difficulties, both physical and mental, that lie ahead. I'd be kidding myself to say there isn't some feeling of trepidation as I observe how difficult it can be to grow old. John and I have watched as dear friends have steadily weakened physically and yet, with courage, continued to stay mentally alert and active. As my late mother-in-law used to say, "Growing old is not for sissies." But she also proclaimed that her eighties had been "the best years of her life." Had she not suffered from hip problems, I think she would have lived much longer than her ninety-two years.

John is six years older than I. The male life expectancy is six years less than that of a female. But that doesn't take into account the extent to which self-care and modern medicine come into play. John's health is superb. His diet is remarkably restrained and for years he has walked miles every day. I am learning to take better care of myself, to foist fewer obligations on myself, and to allow more time for relaxation. I view each day as a gift, no longer believing as I once did that my life was going to be a short one. My faith gives me a sense of peace about the future, a sense that no matter what lies ahead, even beyond this temporal life, John and I will work to support and care for one another.

# Dialogue on Aging

JOHN: Of the many demands made upon a marriage and any committed relationship, I think, at seventy-one, that aging is one of the trickiest, particularly because for such a long time it is subtle, even imperceptible. We don't like to acknowledge it, and when we do, we try to make light of it. But it does entail increasing demands upon a relationship, calling for a special patience and a sense of humor.

DIANE: So what has happened to you and me in this process of aging? When you and I were married, I was twenty-three, and now I'm sixty-five and you're seventy-one. What kinds of changes have we seen in each other? I know that I've seen my pace at the office slow down a little, even as I try to keep doing everything I have to do. I also realize that when I come home, I feel more exhausted than I used to feel, and I'm sure that shows in my face and body. I wonder how that makes you feel, not only about me but about yourself?

JOHN: Aging does take its toll upon your lovely body and your lovely face. Of necessity, they don't have the youthfulness they did when you were twenty-five. I would still call you beautiful, but it's a beauty of a somewhat different kind now, because your face does have lines and your body, though lean, is not as supple as it once was. But I have shifted to a fuller appreciation of your person and do not dwell quite so much on the physical aspects, which were important to me and still remain important to me. As for myself, in my twenties and thirties I was a fairly strong man. I had lots of muscle, having worked in a quarry, and I could carry heavy weights. Today I'm unwilling to carry a case of wine into the house, for fear it might do something to my back, so when I take the wine bottles out of the car, I do it in stages, and sometimes you help me. Well, that's a blow to my male vanity, though I don't like to admit it. When we were at the farm recently, I wanted to move a heavy object out of the basement to be put up for auction. The auctioneer, our longtime friend, Gerry Pennay, was with me and suggested we carry the object out of the basement together. I was about to say yes, because that was my macho self speaking. And then I said to myself, "Oh, you might do something really harmful to your back, just say no." So I said no, leaving him to get outside help. But it was difficult to do.

DIANE: It's difficult to see you say no to such things. I recognize how important they've been to your ego. As I said many times, when I first laid eyes on you, you looked like a football player, with strong shoulders, a broad back, and narrow waist and hips. Now, through the years, you've become much slimmer, and you've lost that dimension in your shoulders. But you know what? I see it as a sweet process of change. I see what's happened in your face as a sweetening and softening rather than simply aging. I see you becoming more mellow, not only in your heart but in your body. And that's a transformation I'm quite comfortable with. As for myself, I rarely wear clothes that don't have sleeves, because I don't like my arms to show. I realize my waist is not as narrow as it used to be. And I also realize that my face has lines in it that I never used to see. You know, I used to worry about that and say to myself, "Is Scoop not going to love me anymore because I'm not as pretty as I once was?" And I finally reached the point of thinking, you know, it *doesn't matter.* What *does* matter is that we continue to move through life together, understanding that these kinds of changes are inevitable and accepting them.

JOHN: That's the key. Not only to understand but to accept. I think it would be wrong for me to say it's always easy. It isn't. And I would also emphasize that we're talking about our aging process at a time when our complaints are really quite minor. Whereas five or ten years from now, that may not be the case, and they could be more serious. But yes, it does require an attitudinal change—perhaps an enlargement of love and affection. It occurs to me that at this time of what I would call incipient aging, I still hold to the illusion that our ailments have plateaued, and that they are what they are and won't get more severe. Of course, this is illusory, because even while we think we're on a plateau, our body is in constant decline. The process is inexorable. And I have to ask myself, in all honesty, whether five or ten years from now, assuming we're both here, I will have the same patience, the same sympathy. After all, some of these ailments can be awkward, difficult, even embarrassing.

DIANE: There's another important issue we haven't touched on, and that's what's going on in the world right now. The very discussion of aging makes me feel uncomfortable, in this fall of 2001, with anthrax about us, with the destruction of the World Trade Center just behind us. The world has changed so much that even to think about the aging process is to be optimistic. I don't know whether we're going to be able to live out our lives. I pray that we will. My faith is that we will.

And yet at the same time I fear for the whole world, so how *I* age becomes a minimal concern.

JOHN: I don't share your pessimism. I think five or ten years from now our lifestyle will unquestionably have changed. There'll be greater security measures, both national and international. But my hunch is that most of us will proceed without continuing calamities. I must say I have enormous admiration and respect for ailing friends. For example, a couple with whom we had dinner recently are dealing with ailments far more severe than ours, and they maintain their spirit. I think of another couple, closer to death, who maintain the same spirit of love and affection. That has to be one of the great tests of the durability of a relationship, as it moves toward the end. Can love endure under different circumstances from those it began with? I hope I'm up to that.

DIANE: What do you mean, you hope you're up to that?

JOHN: I hope that I can have the generosity of spirit not only to accept but to continue to support you, Diane, if your physical problems become serious and the day-to-day routine becomes grubby.

DIANE: Grubby?

JOHN: Yes.

DIANE: Do you have doubts about that, in yourself?

JOHN: Yes, I have doubts. But I think of the work I'm doing at the hospice. Watching other people die, as you necessarily do at a hospice, and, at the same time, aware of the love and care that's given to them—that has encouraged me to believe that I can do the same.

DIANE: I agree that caring for a loved one as he or she gets older and loses faculties is a frightening proposition. Thank God you and I haven't come anywhere near that point. We're both still active and enjoying every aspect of life. If there's a fear about aging, I think you've put your finger on it. I think watching someone you love deeply and have loved deeply for many years—watching that person decline has got to be the hardest aspect of keeping that commitment in the heart.

JOHN: I think I'm most afraid of the situation, Diane, in which one of us would be reasonably healthy and the other, without a life-threatening illness, would be considerably less healthy. So there would be a clear disparity in well-being. It might be better if we both went down this road together, with our ailments being more or less equal.

DIANE: At the same time, you have to remember that commitment, in this sense, does mean that if one goes down first, the other will care for the ailing partner and undertake the responsibilities that the ailing one can no longer deal with.

JOHN: I think I will recognize the formal obligation and do my best to discharge it. The question I'm raising is whether, deep down in the heart of me, I will be able to maintain, with the same force as in the past, the affection, the love, the respect. That's a test that I may have to face at some point, and I hope I can succeed.

DIANE: Somehow, watching you over all these years, I'm less doubtful than you about your ability and commitment. Actually, listening to your reports regarding hospice work over the past few months, I've been amazed at how caring your manner has been as you've seen people die. I watched my mother decline, and my father die suddenly, but that was the closest I ever came to experiencing firsthand someone's death. Her care was provided by doctors and nurses, so my willingness to carry out the sad chores occasioned by her decline was never tested. I promise you—and myself—that if a time comes when I am called on to care for *you,* I will do so, to the very best of my ability, with love and kindness.

JOHN: And I make the same promise to you.

# Grandparenting

## John

Diane and I have three grandchildren: Alex, the sixteen-year-old son of Nancy and David; Benjamin, the three-year-old son of Jennie and Russell; and their new baby, Sarah. We have been grandparents for only four years, but already we've begun to savor the special joys of grandparenting. We've also come to understand and accept its proper limitations.

First, I find that I can reach out to my grandchildren with a certain freedom. We come together with few expectations and even fewer obligations. We're simply who we are, and we accept each other on that basis. I find this gives our relationship a liberating quality.

Second, I can afford to be less than responsible in small but delightful ways. As a grandfather, I seem to have acquired a license to spoil my grandchildren as I wish. Thus I can alter a diet, interrupt a schedule, or indulge a whim. I get vicarious pleasure from these infractions, recalling my own delight in upsetting a parental regime. I thrive on these episodes of minor anarchy.

Third, through grandparenting I see myself in an enlivening light. Benjamin at three or Alex at sixteen inevitably calls up images of myself as a baby or an adolescent boy. These images reinforce my conviction that chronological time is largely irrelevant to my inner sense of time. When I'm with them, I'm three or sixteen or somewhere in between. It's in this sense that grandparenting helps keep me young.

At the same time, Diane and I have imposed certain limitations upon our grandparenting. If we're asked, we will offer advice concerning our grandchildren's upbringing; otherwise we remain on the sidelines, unless the issue seems particularly important. Given the ignorance with which we raised Jennie and David, we are hesitant to offer opinions.

We've also agreed to keep overnight visits to our children's homes to no more than two or three days. Even with the best of intentions on the part of all concerned, the presence of grandparents inevitably puts an additional strain on the parents. These strains are apt to be compounded since, in each case, both of the parents are at work outside the house. It is up to the parents, therefore, to set the date of arrival—and of departure.

Has our marriage been enhanced by the presence of these grandchildren in our lives? I think so, because grandparenting has proven to be a joint experience for us. Together we share activities with our grandchildren, such as playing, talking, shopping, and eating. As a couple, we rejoice in their startling growth, take pride in their accomplishments, and express gratitude for their lives. I think Diane and I have found that in reaching out to our grandchildren, we also reach out to each other in new and unexpected ways.

I would cite silliness as an example. Normally Diane and I

are fairly serious people, but we do engage in a certain amount of playfulness. Now, however, we are allowed by their parents, and indeed encouraged by our grandchildren, to be silly with them. In turn, I believe that these days Diane and I are more apt to be silly with each other. Something of their youth has happily rubbed off on us.

# Diane

Everything I write now is under the shadow of September 11, 2001. I am particularly worried for the future of my grandchildren, those here among us now and those to come. I'm worried about the kind of world they will experience, or—my most drastic worry—whether the world will actually continue to exist. My anxiety knows no bounds.

These young people, whether they are sixteen, three, or yet to be born, will live an extraordinarily different life from that of their parents or grandparents. I lived through World War II, the war in Korea, and the U.S. operation in Vietnam, and never felt that my personal security was threatened by a foreign entity, with one exception: during the Cuban missile crisis, when I feared the United States might be drawn into a full-scale nuclear war with the Soviet Union. Once the drama of those few weeks had passed, I had faith that our government would protect and defend us and that we were a mighty nation equipped with the necessary intelligence and armaments to keep our country safe.

Now, in the aftermath of September 11, I realize that those days of security belong to a different era in a different century. The words "peaceful" and "tranquil," I fear, will not be ones historians use to describe America early in the twenty-first century.

Putting those gloomy thoughts aside, I can confirm that what they say about a grandparent's relationship with an infant grandchild is absolutely true: you fall in love. From the first moment I laid eyes on Benjamin, that beautiful boy, I knew my life was changed. Far from concerns about the responsibilities of parenthood, I completely adored and accepted this child, as both a physical and spiritual being. I became magically entranced by his eyes, his mouth, his nose, his fingers and toes. Holding him in my arms felt like an act of holiness. To watch his responses, to hear Jennie and Russell interpret his needs based on his tiniest gestures was a marvel. As he has grown now to the age of three, I realize what a solid foundation of security he has been given by his parents, and how fortunate a child he is for that gift.

Our son, David, married his lovely wife, Nancy, after she had had a son by a prior marriage. John and I met Alex when he was twelve, just entering adolescence, appropriately questioning everything that was happening around him, especially, perhaps, this new set of grandparents he had suddenly acquired.

The learning process for me has been slower with Alex, now sixteen, a brilliant young man who possesses charm, good looks, and the ability to articulate complex ideas. I remember David and Jennie at that age, both wanting their space—especially from me—and making no bones about it. Alex has been more generous, allowing me to become part of his life with kindness and gentleness. He's willing to help me in the kitchen, for example, a task he performs happily and well. We talk about the radio business and what it's like to do a daily broadcast. He's interested in—and good at—computers, and we share information about the Internet. Right now he wants to learn about Japanese art, so John has had an opportunity to share his knowledge of the Japanese works in the Freer Gallery. All these instances provide opportunities for growth in the relationship between Alex and his new set of grandparents.

Our experiences with Alex are different from those we've had with Benjamin and Sarah, yet we regard them all as our grandchildren. Since we've come into each relationship from different directions, I suspect we'll share our lives with them in different ways. When you come into a twelve-year-old's life, he is already his own person. When you're introduced to a child from birth, there's more of an opportunity to play a role in the formation of his ideas and his outlook. Having said that, I know that we'll do everything we can to support Alex as he finishes high school and embarks on a new academic experience at the college level. I have a sense that our relationship with each other will grow and change every bit as much as our relationship with Benjamin and Sarah will be transformed through their growing years.

Grandparenting is a privilege I was afraid I would never live to experience. Having come this far, I'm now allowing myself to be excited about how my life will be intertwined with the lives of these young people, and the extent to which I can contribute to their moral and spiritual growth.

## Dialogue on Grandparenting

JOHN: September 11 has certainly changed our lives in many ways, including my attitude toward my grandchildren. Before September 11, I could say that having them was a totally joyous experience, in the full confidence that they would have a good opportunity to lead long and satisfying lives. Today, that assumption seems naive and perhaps even inaccurate. Who can know the environment in which they will be living five or ten years from now? The joy of grandparenting is now offset by a new sobriety and concern, and, beyond that, fear.

DIANE: I feel anxiety moving through me sharply as we conduct this dialogue on grandparenting. I feel helpless. I feel as though no matter how I love and support each of these children, it's all out of my hands and control. At the same time, I have to be positive and supportive. I realize that my anxieties can't be allowed to overshadow what we experience with these children, or else they too will feel nothing but fear, and I certainly don't want that to happen. At the same time, I don't know how to react anymore. I'm fearful.

JOHN: The fear is eminently understandable and sane. But yes, I think it's terribly important that we treat these grandchildren as we would have before September 11, that is, giving them love and encouragement and trying in small ways— because grandparents can't do a great deal—to strengthen the wholesome values we know they're acquiring from their parents.

DIANE: Moving away from all that fear and anxiety, how does being a grandparent seem to you different from being a parent?

JOHN: As a parent, I had and still have an immediate responsibility toward our children. They're mature adults now, but in small ways I still exercise that parental responsibility. In the case of our grandchildren, as I said in my essay, there is a delicious *ir*responsibility, not to be carried too far, to be sure, but a freedom to play with them, to cavort with them—and to be serious with them. Also, although recognizing that the influence cannot be as great as that of their parents, trying to remain a part of their moral and spiritual life, as well as just having good fun.

DIANE: I ask myself to what extent we should be involved in disciplining our grandchildren. There are times when I feel that I have a right to speak out and say something about a particular behavior that doesn't please me. And I do say things to each of them. I try to say them gently, and I say them in a different way from the way I said such things to our own children. What about you?

JOHN: Well, I think there is a kind of disciplining that can be properly and wisely exercised by grandparents. But I must say, for me the key word is caution. First of all, I don't think we can have *that* much influence on our grandchildren, because they're in a daily environment of which we're not a part. Beyond that, in consideration of, and respect for, the role the parents play in the lives of their children, I think the discipline must be marginal, peripheral if you will. It may be undertaken from time to time, to be sure, but always, if possible, with deference, either explicit or implicit, to the parents. Ultimately, of course, the parents are in charge.

DIANE: I also wonder how generous we should be as grandparents. It's all so different from my role as parent. Of course, I wanted to make sure that our kids had what they needed, but with our grandchildren I feel as though—and perhaps it's because we're in a different, more settled place materially—I want to give them everything we possibly can. I'm sure age has something to do with it. You can't take anything to the grave with you, and I want to make sure that these grandchildren are generously but carefully taken care of.

JOHN: I like the use of the word "carefully." One can be quite generous in monetary and similar ways with one's grandchildren, but at the same time, my hope would be to instill values unrelated to the material world—honesty, decency, compassion. If they're in reasonable balance, then I think one can afford to be fairly generous with one's grandchildren without spoiling them, in the sense of not making them too attached to material goods.

DIANE: Do you find the display of affection easier with Benjamin at age three than you did with David and Jennie at age three?

JOHN: Oh yes, I think so. With respect to our children, a show of affection tended to take place—for me at least—in a context of overall parental responsibility. Maybe I had concerns about too little or too much expression of warmth and love. In the case of our grandchildren, I'm largely freed of those preoccupations, and I can hug and kiss with a certain abandon. That's one of the joyous aspects of grandparenting.

DIANE: I think I felt more free than you did in hugging and kissing and playing with them when they were infants and children. I think you needed to wait until they were almost five or six before you really got into it. As they grew older, you were more able to relate to them. Now I see you with Benjamin, holding him in ways that I don't think you held David.

JOHN: Your memory is better than mine. I certainly sense an ease and freedom in holding Benjamin, playing with him, and talking with him, because he has his own vocabulary now, though it's not always intelligible to his grandparents. That's a special quality of being a grandparent. But I do want to make one point: it's easy for us to talk about the joys of being grandparents, but we couldn't be as close to our grandchildren unless a really solid foundation had been created by their parents. I trust we will see these three children becoming the responsible and caring adults we would want them to be.

DIANE: I like the ways we stay in touch with our grandchildren. We have the chance to speak with and visit Alex fairly often, but I find myself yearning to see Benjamin and Sarah more often, because these are the years they are growing and changing so rapidly. The photographs that Jennie and Russell send regularly are wonderful, but I want to see the kids and their parents more frequently.

JOHN: Among the many consequences of September 11, 2001, will be a greater sensitivity to occasions when we can get together. I think we'll find ourselves planning reunions of one kind or another more deliberately. As many commentators have said—and I think quite rightly—September 11 has made us more aware of being alive—

DIANE: —and of the people we love.

# Death

## John

As I grow older, I find myself confronting death more often—
my death and that of others. The obituary page has ceased to
be irrelevant. The number of funerals and memorial services I
attend has grown. I've even begun to select the hymns I would
like sung at my memorial service.

All of these encounters with death leave unanswered, of
course, the transcendent questions, namely, what will my death
mean? Will it be no more than a cessation of bodily functions?
Will it entail a new form of continuing life? And will I, as my
finite self, experience some intimation of that life?

Recently I've become aware of yet another aspect of death.
This is what I call the priority of death in a marriage or comparable relationship. It is a virtual certainty that, barring some
catastrophe, either Diane or I will predecease the other. We have
discussed this eventuality only sporadically. Diane will say, for
example, "Don't you dare leave me alone." Or, anticipating *her*
death before mine, "Make sure that the paintings and furniture

are passed on to Jennie and David." In Diane's mind and perhaps mine as well, the prospect of being the surviving spouse
seems its own kind of death.

What is at stake is the demise not only of one's partner but of
the partnership itself. A marriage is, I think, successful to the
extent that its participants consciously create the entity that
binds them together. That entity is more than what each partner
brings to it. An uncommitted relationship entails no more than
cohabitation. A committed relationship demands a collabora-
tion in order to develop and endure.

Over the centuries, some of the best minds have clung to the
hope of somehow communicating with a deceased spouse. I
have no such illusion. If I survive Diane, however, I'll be able
to draw on a rich bank of memories. Admittedly, such memories stir mixed feelings. On the one hand, they can dull the
sharpness of separation; on the other, they can freshen the sadness of loss.

All of which intensifies my determination to continue celebrating Diane's and my partnership. That celebration regards
each day as a gift—not to be slighted or taken for granted. And
as a gift, it is of infinite value, oblivious to the finitude of coming
days.

# Diane

When I was a little girl, I remember telling my mother over and
over again that I didn't want her to die before I did. In my childhood imagination, I simply could not picture life without my

mother in it. Even with all the difficulties I experienced as her daughter, I never wanted her to leave me behind.

As I look ahead to a time that's approaching—who can know when or where—either John or I will almost certainly leave this earth before the other. I feel sad at anticipating our parting, and now more apprehensive as well, as we live through the events since September 11, 2001. John and I have shared so much that I have a hard time imagining not having him by my side to talk over and remember the experiences, the mistakes, the good times, and the small things. Even now, after all these years of marriage, if I awaken earlier than John and the sky is particularly beautiful, I want him to come to the window and see it with me. If I'm in the garden alone and there's a sweet new rose in bloom, I call John to come and share it with me. We take long walks together, watching the young children in the neighborhood trying out their two-wheelers, and almost simultaneously we remember watching Jennie train herself to ride a unicycle, getting back on each time she fell off, determined to master it. Or, as we watch a young neighbor's boy grow into manhood, and see him drive away in his family's car, recalling David's excitement and seriousness when he received his own first car. So many memories. Simple things, like reading the newspaper together on Sunday mornings, each of us pointing out a story to the other, exclaiming with wonder over one item, reacting with horror at another. Each of those moments I am holding in my memory, because I fear that someday, that may be all I have of him.

Over the years, I've interviewed many widows who have written about the experience of losing a spouse. By the time they're finally able to write about the loss, most of the extreme forms of sadness are past. But what I've found interesting is the amount of *anger* that remains, not because of what went on in the marriage but because the husband has simply *died*. The widow has been left behind, to grieve, mourn, and try to figure out the rest of her life.

Because I've been professionally involved in an extremely demanding job for more than twenty years, I know how much I've come to depend on John to carry out many of the details that keep our lives running smoothly. He watches over me, and he reminds me to take care of myself. I ask myself whether I will be willing and able to fill in all the gaps he would leave behind, should he die before me. And I ask myself, if I *am* left behind, will I remain engaged in life with the joy and enthusiasm I have come to know in the past few years? Or without his support will I withdraw into myself?

My father died less than a year after my mother died. I've always believed he died of a broken heart. Now that John and I have lived together in this marriage for forty-two years, I can better understand why.

## Dialogue on Death

DIANE: I think the older I get, the less afraid I become of death. I think I fear *your* death, or that of someone close to me, more than I fear my own. The notion of death as a long sleep that doesn't have an end doesn't frighten me. Of course, I would love to see our grandchildren grow into adulthood. I'd love to be present at their marriages, if that's what they choose.

JOHN: I have a strong sense of the unreality of death. Death is preeminently a subject that puts the heart in opposition to the mind. Rationally, of course, I know that I will die and that you will die, but I really can't deal with that contingency. Death is an abstraction that doesn't carry much weight, and particularly today. As we look out over our beautiful garden on this superb autumnal afternoon, the idea of death seems remote indeed. But I agree with you that it's harder to contemplate the death of those in the family, children as well as spouse, and particularly the notion of having to spend what might be a significant part of life without the other. That's a kind of death that may be more difficult than one's own dying.

DIANE: All of us probably fear a long and painful illness that takes us to the end of life without dignity and the presence of those we love. I'm determined that that's not going to happen to me. I feel that I can have a measure of control over my end. I agree with you that life after the other spouse's death would not be easy and would require a remaking of one's day-to-day existence, without the companionship and warmth that have become so important to both of us, especially as we've grown older. But I must say my faith tells me that all those we love will be together, in some way, in some form, after life has ended. My belief tells me that life, in all its forms, is ongoing. We'll perceive each other's presence, even as we move along in our own lives.

JOHN: That raises an idea I've been kicking around. Normally, as we think of a dead person—and particularly a dead spouse—we try to console ourselves with the notion that we can draw on memories to keep us going and maintain the relationship. But that's a matter of constantly looking backward. I wonder if there's a way of looking *forward,* and although the spouse is dead, nevertheless being able to—this may sound a little crazy—establish an active relationship in which the deceased spouse enters into a kind of conversation with the surviving spouse. It would be more than drawing upon passive memories; it would involve conducting an *ongoing* relationship of a kind.

DIANE: Give me an example. Do you mean that if one has a big decision to make—to sell a house, say, or move elsewhere—one begins to conduct a dialogue that might have gone on with the spouse?

JOHN: Actually, I hadn't been thinking in practical terms. I had in mind more of a spiritual conversation, although it would turn on the events of the world and the events of my life. But I wouldn't preclude a conversation where one seeks help or enlightenment from the deceased spouse.

DIANE: I guess one of the basic questions that individuals who've been together for a long time ask each other is: Would you marry again after my death, or would I marry again after your death? How do you answer the question?

JOHN: I don't have any fundamental objection. It's often been said that if the surviving spouse is interested in a new marriage, that's evidence that the first relationship was successful and afforded a healthy foundation for a second relationship.

The notion that remarriage is disloyal is something I've never agreed with.

Diane: I take the view that learning to live with someone over forty-two years has been a long, rich, and vital process. My question would be how much of that learning I would be able to bring to another relationship, and I'm not sure what the answer is.

John: I think the patience, sensitivity, and willingness to share thoughts engendered by the first relationship would all go to provide a good basis for the next relationship.

Diane: At the same time, I find myself thinking in another direction, especially because I've rarely been alone in my life, except for the year between the time I was divorced and you and I were married. I wonder what it would be like to be alone, to make decisions for myself and not have to take into account someone else's desires. I'm not saying that I know which way I'd go, but that's something else that comes into my mind. I love your idea of somehow finding a way to have conversations in the future, whether they're about practical things or whether they're simply a joining of minds.

John: As for living alone, of course I've done a lot of that. It was true in college when, after my freshman year, I had my own room. In law school I was essentially alone. Before our marriage, I had several years of living alone here in Washington. In a sense, it might be too easy for me to resume a life alone. I think I might be drawn to the idea of a second relationship, assuming the circumstances were propitious.

Diane: You know, it's really interesting to see the extent to which you and I have almost exchanged positions. I'm the one who for so long fought against being alone, and you're the one who for so long *insisted* on being alone. Now, after all these years of marriage, as we contemplate the end of the life of the other spouse, we've somehow changed positions on that.

JOHN: Yes, to some extent I think we have. I'm struck by this conversation, because we've begun to sketch out—and I don't think you and I have ever done this before—some of our thoughts about how the survivor could have a rewarding life even after the death of his or her spouse. There may be more life after the death of the spouse than I had thought about to this point.

DIANE: It's long been said that women are the survivors. Women can and do live as widows for many many years. Men, on the other hand, need the companionship, and therefore men tend to marry again—or at least establish new relationships—fairly quickly, because they're uncomfortable without having that other person in their lives.

JOHN: I think that may be a passing phenomenon. It goes back to a time when men really didn't have much ability or talent to take care of themselves.

DIANE: I think there are *still* men like that. . . .

JOHN: Yes, but I think they're a declining number. There are more men who are able to care for themselves.

DIANE: Does this conversation make you uncomfortable?

JOHN: No, surprisingly not. But I really have to come back to my first point. It's deceptively easy to talk about death when—although it could occur tomorrow or in the next minute—it's still fairly remote. If you and I were having this conversation when both of us were seriously ill, I think we'd be talking in somewhat different ways.

DIANE: I think you're absolutely right. Therefore I want to come back to something I said in my essay. I really do cherish each and every minute that you and I have, and I hope that we will have many more years together.

JOHN: And I would simply add that you and I are both sensitive to the need to celebrate each day as a gift, because that's what it is.

# Conclusion

We wrote most of this book under idyllic circumstances. We were able to take advantage of a long, uninterrupted vacation at our farm in a remote area of northeastern Pennsylvania. Most days we were entirely by ourselves, deep in the quiet and—as visitors invariably sense—the magic of the place.

We quickly established what proved to be a productive regime. We got up at the deliciously late hour of 7:30 a.m. After a leisurely breakfast, we spent a good three hours or so writing and editing essays and conducting and recording dialogues, which Diane would then transcribe. After lunch outside on the patio, we devoted the afternoon to long walks, work around the house, and reading. Diane also used this time to stay in touch with her office through a battery of electronic equipment. We concluded the day with dinner—often before an open fire—and the amusement of a favorite video. Then to bed around 10:00 p.m., anticipating another fruitful tomorrow. Even at the time, we knew how precious these days were, and how their memory would be cherished.

Writing this book has been a journey of unexpected pleasure, as well as learning, for both of us. To be sure, along the way we've dealt with dark and painful episodes in our marriage. But we've also illumined some of the enduring strengths of our relationship. We've tried to address each topic fairly and honestly, in both the essays and the dialogues.

The process has brought us closer together. It's demonstrated our ability to collaborate effectively over particularly sensitive terrain. We've respected each other's views, and we've acknowledged our disagreements as well as agreements. A joint authorship can be a hazardous enterprise, especially since humans invest so much of themselves in the written word. We've been happily surprised by the relative ease with which we settled on the text of each topic.

Moreover, writing the book has given us the mutual opportunity to say to each other, "Thank you for sustaining our marriage, and forgive me for letting you and the marriage down at times." The very act of staying together for over forty years implies, we think, such gratitude and forgiveness. But this book represents a particularly enduring way of expressing such forms of love and therefore love itself.

Now, out of the struggles we've had, some successful, others not successful, we would modestly offer four suggestions toward promoting a long-lasting relationship.

1. Communicate feelings as well as thoughts to your partner. The most rational dialogue can miss the point if both partners are not sharing their feelings. Moreover, such sharing will strengthen the relationship, since it will reveal more of the partners' true selves.

2. Respect your partner's sensitivities and frailties. In many ways, adults are essentially children who put on a variety of masks for different occasions. Their presumed maturity is a pose that conceals the unavoidable anxieties that spring

from childhood. In order to understand your partner, you should embrace his or her internal child.

3. Be patient with your partner. Patience captures several aspects of a vital relationship—that is, acceptance, compassion, and constancy. Patience presumes that you embrace your partner's entire personality. By being patient, you are sharing the pain your partner will unavoidably suffer at times. Through patience, you are displaying your enduring loyalty to your partner.

4. With your partner, use this book and, in particular, the questions in the appendix as a springboard for pursuing the issues in your relationship. You might do so by combining, as we have done, written thoughts and oral exchanges. By whatever means, do your best to share your joys and pains, your strengths and weaknesses with your partner, in the confidence that love thrives on mutual understanding.

In the final analysis, is marriage or a comparable long-term commitment worthwhile? Not for everyone, to be sure. Some may try it and find it unrewarding. Others may not wish to undertake such a commitment at all. Still others, like us, have found that the joys of an intimate and sustained relationship outweigh the disappointments. Would either of us have wanted a less difficult and problematic marriage? Of course. Would either of us have preferred a different spouse? Emphatically no.

We have written this book in the belief that an honest account of a marriage of more than forty years may encourage other marriages and comparable relationships not only to endure, but to flourish.

# Appendix

## QUESTIONS FOR READERS

### Assumptions and Expectations

- What assumptions do you bring to our relationship?
- What are your expectations of yourself as a partner?
- What are your expectations of me?

### Appeal

- What are the qualities about me that most appeal to you?
- What aspects of my personality are most attractive to you?
- What aspects of my personality bother you?

### Anger

- How did your parents deal with anger in your family?
- What issues would anger them?
- How did your parents express anger toward you?
- What makes you angry?
- What do you do when you get angry?

## Family

- What was the relationship between your mother and father?
- How did their relationship affect you as you grew up?
- What kind of a relationship did you have with your sibling(s)?
- What kind of a relationship did your parents have with your sibling(s)?

## Making Love

- Do you feel good about sex?
- How many sexual partners have you had?
- Have you been disappointed in prior sexual partners? If so, why?
- How important a factor do you believe sex is in our relationship?
- Do you have expectations about how frequently we will have sex?

## Solitude

- How important is solitude for you?
- How much time do you like to spend alone?
- Can you tell me when you need time alone?
- Can we accommodate each other's need for solitude versus time together?

## Money

- Was your family frugal or generous in dealing with money?
- As you were growing up, how freely could you spend money?
- How will we handle our money?
- How will we deal with debt?
- Will we consolidate our incomes?

## Profession

- How did your parents' professional lives affect you?
- How happy are you in your working life?
- What do you like and dislike about your work?
- How much of a role will you expect me to play in your professional life?
- How will you balance your professional and home life?

## Religion

- Did your family actively participate in church activities?
- Did you grow up as a churchgoer?
- Will you be an active churchgoer?
- To what extent will you expect our children (if any) to be part of a church?

## Parenting

- Do you want to have children?
- What are the primary memories you have of your own parents?
- What were their strengths and weaknesses?
- What are your expectations of yourself as a parent?
- What measures would you use to discipline a child?

## Arguing

- What is your view of the purpose of arguing?
- How important is it to you to win an argument?
- How would you describe your style of arguing?
- Do you believe that arguing can be constructive?

## Friends

- How important are friends in your life?
- How many good friends would you say you have?
- What do you expect of your friends?
- How would you want me to engage with your friends?

## Vacations

- For you, what makes a good—or bad—vacation?
- Do you like to vacation alone?
- Do you plan ahead or make last-minute decisions?
- Do you think of vacation planning as a shared exercise?

## Criticism

- Did your parents criticize you? If so, how much?
- Do you feel I criticize you a little or a lot?
- What prompts you to criticize me?
- What happens to you when I criticize you?
- Does criticism help or hurt our relationship?

## Psychotherapy

- Do you have fixed views about whether therapy can help people?
- Have you been in therapy?
- If so, how do you think your therapy has affected our relationship?
- If I felt the need, would you consider therapy for the two of us?

## Retirement

- Do you intend to retire?
- If so, do you anticipate retirement with pleasure or anxiety?
- What activities would you take up in retirement?
- How do you see our life together when we both retire?

## The Other Partner as Professional

- Are you comfortable with my career?
- If my status and income should exceed yours, would it trouble you?

- If we have children and maintain our careers, how will we handle our parenting responsibilities?
- Can we share the pressures of our careers with each other?

## Holiday Celebrations

- What are your childhood memories of holidays?
- Were holidays happy or sad for you?
- Do you now have any special anxieties about holidays?
- If so, how can we address them?

## Illness

- How did your parents deal with their own illnesses?
- Were they sympathetic to your illnesses?
- How do you react to the illness of someone close to you?
- How do you deal with yourself when you are ill?
- How would you like me to care for you when you are ill?

## Food

- What are your most vivid childhood memories about food?
- What foods do you particularly like and dislike?
- Do you enjoy trying new foods?
- Are you comfortable working in the kitchen, either preparing food or cleaning up?
- Do you think you eat sensibly?

## In-Laws

- How would you describe your relationship to my family?
- How much do you anticipate my family will be a part of our lives?
- How frequently will you be willing to visit or spend time with them?
- If problems arise between your family and me, how will you handle them?

## Sleep

- Are you a heavy or a light sleeper?
- How important is it to you to share a bed with your partner?
- Would you be upset if I slept in a separate bed or a separate room?
- How much would that take away from our romance?

## The Third Person

- How important is the idea of fidelity to you?
- How would you react if I were strongly attracted to someone else?
- Would we be able to talk with each other about the attraction?
- What would you do if you found yourself attracted to someone else?
- If I insisted you give up that relationship for our sake, would you do so?
- If necessary, would you agree to seek counseling?

## Aging

- What are the aspects of aging that trouble you the most?

- How important is a youthful appearance to you?

- How do you think you will deal with the infirmities of old age?

- Are there some aspects of aging to which you look forward?

- Are you more concerned about confronting my aging or yours?

## Grandparenting

- Are you excited by the prospect of grandparenting?

- How do you see yourself as a grandparent?

- How might that be different from your role as a parent?

- How will you ensure respect for the parents' primary authority?

## Death

- If your parents are no longer living, how did their deaths affect you?

- How much do you think about your own death?

- Do you intend to make preparations for your own death?

- Will you share those with me?

- If I die before you, would you consider another partner?

# Acknowledgments

There are so many people who have guided us and helped us along our never-ending journey toward understanding the true meaning of commitment. Their efforts during these past forty-two years have helped give us the courage to write this book.

Maxine Thornton Denham and John Denham enabled us to begin our dialogue. Jack Harris demonstrated the strength it takes to face adulthood. And now Susan Fiester continues to steer us through the changing landscape of our lives.

It has been our good fortune to share our lives with many friends who've provided love, support, and understanding. They've helped us to realize that we have not been alone in our struggles.

Robert Gottlieb has been an invaluable editor and critic, as well as a good friend.

At Knopf, thanks to Katy Barrett, Paul Bogaards, Tracy Cabanis, Kathleen Fridella, Katherine Hourigan, Pat Johnson, Sonny Mehta, Jill Morrison, Bonnie Schiff-Glenn, Virginia Tan, and Abby Weintraub.

Finally, the greatest gift in our lives has been our children, David and Jennie, who challenged us, who forced us to grow, and who are now living their own lives of commitment—to their spouses, to their children, and to society.

A NOTE ABOUT THE AUTHORS

Diane Rehm has hosted *The Diane Rehm Show* on WAMU and National Public Radio since 1979. Currently it is distributed by NPR and American Forces Radio Network to cities across the country and around the world. John B. Rehm, a Washington attorney specializing in international trade, both in government and private practice, is retired. Diane and John live in Bethesda, Maryland.

A NOTE ON THE TYPE

This book was set in Granjon, a type named in compliment to Robert Granjon, a type cutter and printer active in Antwerp, Lyons, Rome, and Paris from 1523 to 1590. Granjon, the boldest and most original designer of his time, was one of the first to practice the trade of typefounder apart from that of printer. Linotype Granjon was designed by George W. Jones, who based his drawings on a face used by Claude Garamond (ca. 1480–1561) in his beautiful French books. Granjon more closely resembles Garamond's own type than do any of the various modern faces that bear his name.

Composed by NK Graphics, Keene, New Hampshire
Printed and bound by R. R. Donnelley & Sons,
Crawfordsville, Indiana
Designed by Virginia Tan